A GUIDE TO CLUB LAW AND PRACTICE

Robert Upex

MA LLM ACIArb Barrister

Professor of Law (Emeritus) at the University of Surrey

Former Employment Judge

Published June 2025 by

Spiramus Press Ltd
102 Blandford Street
London W1U 8AG
www.spiramus.com

ISBN
9781913507718   Paperback
9781913507725   Digital

British Library Cataloguing-in-Publication Data.

A catalogue record for this book is available from the British Library.

Contents

Preface

The number of clubs and associations in this country is vast. The activities they cover are wide-ranging – from small local choral societies or knitting circles with a small membership to well-known national organisations with a large membership. They include clubs like the Kennel Club, the Women's Institute, Rotary, and the Hurlingham Club. Some of them are to be found all over the country – for example, the WI has branches in many towns and villages. Many towns and villages also have sports clubs – for playing golf, tennis, squash and athletics, amongst others. The common feature of all these organisations is their legal status: they are all classified by the Law as "unincorporated associations", irrespective of their size. This legal status means that they are outside the regulatory framework to which organisations like companies (which are *incorporated*) are subject. The law in this area comes mainly from cases, not legislation; some of the cases date from the 19th century.

I have sat on the committee of various clubs, ranging from social clubs to professional associations. When the members of the club or association are like-minded and pursue the same objectives, without disagreement, all proceeds smoothly. When there is dissension, it is then that the law comes into play and the different groups start looking at the legal position. But where to start? The starting-point – and the core of the club's being – is its Constitution or Rules. These are the bedrock of the club and form the basis upon which it operates. If they are clear and well-drafted, then the members will find a way of dealing with the issue. If they are unclear, litigation in the courts is on the horizon. Many of the cases which have been decided in this area have arisen from ambiguities in a club's rules. Those cases form the background to understanding a club's rules and interpreting them.

The aim of the book is to provide a guide to this area of the law. There are large reference works available, but they are for lawyers. This book is not directed at them. It is for well-informed non-lawyers who need a guide which they can understand without having to cope with legal jargon. Its main aim is to help those who are involved in the management and running of a club and who need to be aware of the possible pitfalls that may occur and the risks to which they may be exposed.

In the course of writing this book I have been helped in different ways by a number of friends and colleagues. I am particularly grateful to Ian Bracey, David Gregory, Stephen Hardy, Ian Martin, Christine and Peter Teasdale and Mary and Roger Sleigh. Their help has been invaluable. Needless to say, I am responsible for any errors or omissions.

The law is stated as at 1 March 2025.

ROBERT UPEX

Introduction

0.1　This book is intended to be a guide to the law relating to clubs. A "club" basically consists of a group of people who come together for social – as opposed to – commercial purposes. They come together to play golf or tennis or bridge, to sing, to do knitting or embroidery. They may be large or small, they may exist in a village or operate on a national scale. They range from the choral society in a small town to well-known organisations such as the Kennel Club or the Garrick Club. They embrace Women's Institutes, Round Tables, Freemasons and Synagogues. They may call themselves a Club, a Circle, an Institute, an Association, a Guild or a Society. What they have in common is their legal status. They are all what the law calls "unincorporated associations". They are also very numerous and are to be found in towns and villages up and down the land. This book is about this group.

0.2　Apart from unincorporated associations, there are other legal structures. These structures are also organisations which are formed for various purposes but they are different creatures. Some of them are mentioned briefly here for the purpose of making clear the difference between them and a club. Here are some examples:

- Charities
- Companies
- Trusts

0.3　A *charity* is an organisation set up for charitable purposes under the Charities Act 2011. It is governed by the Charities Commission. Some clubs may have charitable purposes. In that case, they will be registered as a charity. But that fact will not change their legal structure. They will remain a club, despite the fact that they also have charitable objectives and purposes. The implications of registration as a charity are outside the scope of this book. But it should be noted that a club which has charitable status will be governed by its own rules but will also be under the supervision of the Charities Commission.

0.4   A *company* is a body which is said to be "incorporated". It means that a group of people decide to form a company for commercial, rather than social, purposes. Once incorporated, the company has its own separate legal personality. It will be called X Ltd (if it is a private company) or Y plc (if its shares are quoted on the Stock Exchange). When a company is formed – or incorporated – the fact that it has a separate legal personality means that liability for acts done in its name and on its behalf falls on the company itself. If it is unable to meet its liabilities, it will face liquidation. It is subject to restrictions imposed by and under the Companies Act 2006. An unincorporated association, on the other hand, is generally free from statutory supervision. It is not free, though, from liability under, for example, the Equality Act 2010 in relation to acts of unlawful discrimination whether the alleged victim is a member of the club or an employee of the club or a visitor to the club. Also, because the club or association is not incorporated, any liability that arises will in theory fall on all the members. Since the association is not a company, there is no separate legal status for the members to shelter behind to limit their liability.

0.5   A *trust* is also different from an unincorporated association. Traditionally, trusts were used to make provision for families and to pass property and wealth from generation to generation. When a trust is set up, the property within the trust (the "trust property") is held by trustees on trust for those intended to benefit over the generations (the "beneficiaries"). Those who decided to form clubs did not resort to a trust model. A trust only becomes relevant in the case where a club owns or leases its premises. But that is all.

0.6   Some organisations use the word "club", but they are not really clubs in the sense used in this book. Examples are:

- Video clubs
- Health clubs
- Supporters' clubs
- "Friends"

0.7   In the first case, a person becomes a member simply to enable them to hire films. In the second, they pay a joining fee and/or monthly subscription to give them access to the exercise facilities. In the third case, they pay so that they can receive information about the team. In the fourth case – which is similar to the third – they pay to receive information about forthcoming events and to gain priority access to certain events. It is a characteristic of all these "clubs" that so-called membership does not depend on any form of selection and that the members of the "club" have no relationship with each other. They do not have any form of *control* over the running of the club. On the other hand, clubs of the sort considered in this book are organisations which have some method of selection or election and where the members do have a relationship with each other. That relationship is based on the contract of membership, as we shall see. These types of club are controlled by their members.

0.8 Clubs divide into a number of groups. First, there are those which do not own or lease their own premises, probably because they do not need premises to carry out their activities. A choral society, for example, may hire school premises for their rehearsals and then the local church for their concert. On the other hand, sports clubs need to have premises for their activities. Golf clubs, tennis clubs, and squash clubs, for example, are likely to own or lease their premises. Clubs in this category will have to deal with third parties – for example, employing staff to man the premises and engaging contractors to deal with maintenance issues.

0.9 Some clubs may also have to satisfy other requirements to enable them to obtain access to benefits or advantages offered. For example, sports clubs may decide to apply to become Community Amateur Sports Clubs to enable them to obtain tax advantages offered under the Corporation Tax Act 2010. But this possibility is only available to clubs which are engaged in physical sports, as opposed to sports such as chess. A club which is eligible under the Act will have the structure of an unincorporated association but will need to make sure that its rules are also aligned to enable it to comply with the Act's requirements.

0.10 Another group of clubs are so-called "proprietary clubs". These are clubs which are owned by an individual or a company. A member of such a club pays a subscription (and, probably, entrance fee) to be a member of the club. Even if the club has rules and a committee which vets applicants for membership, such a club is different from a non-proprietary club (often called a private members' club) because the individual member has no control over the way it is run. In addition, the proprietor owns the premises, furniture and stock which is made available to the members and in return for the use of which they pay their subscription. In the case of a private members' club, on the other hand, the members own the premises (whether freehold or under a lease), the furniture and the stock. Proprietary clubs are outside the scope of this book.

0.11 This area of the Law is difficult and complex. The purpose of this book is to provide a guide to the main issues which may face a club or association. It is intended for those who become involved in a club, whether as a member or as someone elected to be a member of the Committee which runs the club. There are reference books available which offer detailed guidance on all the legal problems that may arise and these should be consulted for a detailed explanation of any particular issue. The object of *this* book is to offer more general guidance to those who may be best described as "well-informed lay people" – people who do not have legal qualifications and the insights of a professional lawyer.

0.12 The book is divided into four Chapters. The **first** chapter looks at the nature of a club or association, including the legal definition, the Rules or Constitution of the club and the ownership of the club's property. The **second** chapter looks at the members and concentrates on three aspects: admission to the club, treatment of members and termination of membership. The **third** chapter concentrates on the management and running of the club. It looks at the role of the officers and members of the committee and also discusses meetings, which are the forum for the members to discuss the running of the club. The **fourth** chapter considers the relationship of the club with third parties, i.e. those who are not members of the club. The club may incur one of the following forms of liability:

- liability in contract;
- liability in negligence;
- liability as a landlord or tenant;
- other non-criminal liability, such as liability for unlawful discrimination;
- liability under the Health and Safety legislation; and
- criminal liability.

This final chapter goes together with Chapter 3, since any liability that falls on the club will fall, in the first place, on the committee. That raises questions of how the members of the committee may attempt to limit their exposure.

0.13 The term "club" or "clubs" will be used throughout this book. That term means all organisations – whatever their title – which have the legal status of unincorporated associations.

1. The Club

Introduction

1.1   The Chambers Dictionary 2014 gives this definition of a club:

> *"[A]n association of persons for social, political, athletic or other ends; an association of persons who possess premises or facilities which all members may use . . ."*

From this definition three points may be noted:

1.   a number of people (i.e. more than one) is involved;
2.   there must be a reason for their association; and
3.   they may have premises upon which they conduct their activities.

In relation to the second point, it should be noted that the reason for the association should not be a business one. In relation to the third point, the definition makes clear that the possession or ownership of premises is not necessary. Not all clubs will have their own premises. Clearly, a golf club needs to have a golf course so that its members can play golf. A community choir, on the other hand, will almost certainly not own or lease its own premises but will need to hire premises for its concerts. A club with property (owned or leased) is likely to have a wider range of potential obligations than a club which does not: see 1.49.

The legal definition of a Club

1.2   A club has the legal status of an unincorporated association. This means that it consists of a group of people who have not formed themselves into a company; in other words, they have not 'incorporated' themselves. In the case of a company, any legal liability will fall on the company, which is said to have separate legal personality. In the case of a club, on the other hand, since there is no separate legal personality, any legal liability will fall on the members of the club's committee. This matter is discussed at paras. 3.95 to 3.101.

1.3   The generally accepted definition of an unincorporated association is:

> ". . . *two or more persons bound together for one or more common purposes, not being business purposes, by mutual undertakings, each having mutual duties and obligations, in an organisation which has rules which identify in whom control of it and its funds rests and upon what terms and which can be joined or left at will. The bond of union between the members of an unincorporated association has to be contractual.*"

See *Conservative and Unionist Central Office v Burrell* (1982), a Court of Appeal case.

1.4   The following points should be noted about the definition:

- The club must have at least two members
- Those members must have agreed to be bound together for one or more common purposes
- Those purposes should not be business purposes
- The club must have a constitution or rules regulating the behaviour of the members towards each other
- The members of the club have a contract with each other; the terms of the contract are the rules/constitution.

1.5   These last two points are crucial to an understanding of how in law a club works. When a person becomes a member of club he or she enters into a contract. The contract is with all the other members of the club. The terms of the contract – in other words, the member's obligations – are found in the Constitution or Rules of the club. This document sets out the way the club operates and is fundamental to its operation. When there is a dispute, the starting point is the Rules. If they are clear and well-drafted, they should help resolve the dispute.

1.6   The rules of the club are, therefore, extremely important, and should be clearly drafted so as to avoid disputes about what they mean. In the event of a dispute, they should be the place to go to first. It is essential that those drafting the rules think carefully about what to include in them so that they cover likely contingencies. The rules should also be clear and unambiguous. If they are not, that will open the way to disagreements and, ultimately, litigation.

1.7 A contract is an agreement. A person who enters into a contract enters an agreement with others. In the case of a club, the agreement is with the other members of the club. If one of or more of the parties to a contract wish to change its terms, they all have to agree to those changes. In the case of a club, the way to change the terms – the rules – is to change them at a meeting of the members. That is the only way that they may be changed. Changing the rules is discussed further at paras. 1.34 - 1.41, below.

The constitution or rules of the Club

General

1.8 Sometimes the instrument governing the operation of the club is called a "Constitution" and sometimes "Rules". Whatever word is used, the result is the same. The document contains the terms of membership to which all the members are subject and which they must observe. They form the whole basis upon which the club operates and govern the way it conducts its affairs. When a new member joins the club, he or she enters into a contract with all the other members of the club. The terms of the contract entered into thus amount to the new member's obligations towards the other members of the club. The new member enters into the contract when he or she pays the entrance fee (if any) and the first subscription, if there is a rule to that effect. If there is no such rule, the contract will start when the new member is notified of election.

1.9 It is important to be absolutely clear that if the Rules do not deal with a particular point, then the club does not have the power to deal with it. For example, if there is no provision in the Rules for the club's committee to make byelaws or regulations, then the committee does not have that power. The omission can be cured, though. The way to do it is to propose an amendment to the Rules at a meeting of the club members, usually an Extraordinary

General Meeting (EGM). Once the proposed amendment is passed at the meeting, from then on (*but not before*), the committee has the power to make byelaws/regulations. In some cases, it may be possible to argue that a rule should be implied, even though there is no express rule. But that argument only applies in limited circumstances. It is best to have an express rule. See para. 1.25 for a discussion of implied rules.

1.10 Since the Rules contain the terms or obligations which bind a member, they amount to the *express* terms of his or her contract. That being so, the rules should state that the member expressly agrees to be bound by the rules *as made from time to time*. This form of words also caters for possible future changes to the Rules. So, for example, the rules might say something like:

> *"Upon election or admission to the club the member will be subject to its rules and will be provided with a copy of these rules, together with a copy of the club's byelaws. The member shall be bound by all rules and byelaws which may be made from time to time."*

The wording of this draft rule should be noted. It refers to the rules and byelaws "made from time to time". See para. 1.36 for the explanation for this.

1.11 The club's rules regulate the way it operates. To change them, the club needs to go through certain procedures: see para. 1.34 below. The running of the club may be more streamlined if some aspects of its operation are not dealt with by the rules themselves but are dealt with by means of byelaws. So, for example, it may be more convenient for the rules to give the committee the power to set annual subscriptions by byelaws. The advantage of this procedure is that – provided the committee has the power to introduce the byelaws – it is able to set the annual subscription without having to resort to a full meeting of the members. This method makes for greater flexibility and removes the need for the formalities of a General Meeting. On the other hand, though, some clubs may prefer to set the subscription by means of an EGM since the meeting gives the members the opportunity to express their views.

Generally, it makes sense to deal with the day-to-day administration of the club by means of byelaws. These may deal with such matters as the opening times of the club's bar and restaurant (if it has them) and dress codes. It would make little sense to have to call an EGM to change the club's opening hours.

1.12 There is no right answer to these matters. It is up to the club to decide how to regulate its affairs. So, one club may have a rule that byelaws or regulations may only be introduced by a vote of the members in General Meeting; another club may have a rule allowing byelaws or regulations to be introduced by the committee. The differences represent differences in the ways that different clubs choose to regulate themselves. The critical document is the club's rules and what it provides for.

1.13 Those responsible for drafting a club's rules should try to anticipate unexpected eventualities. Take the example of a sports club with valuable premises which were acquired when the club was founded. It has two classes of members: playing members and non-playing social members. It receives an offer from property developers to buy the premises. If the social members are able to outvote the playing members and the premises are sold, the club's sporting objectives will be defeated. It needs to avoid that risk. To achieve that, the club's rules should:

1. limit the number of social members; and
2. state that, in the event of a motion being put to members at a general meeting which is potentially prejudicial to the interests of the playing members, the social members will not be entitled to vote on it.

If the rules did not contain these limitations, the club would be at risk of losing its premises because of the vote of a group of members who did not play the sport which was the main reason for the club's existence. This example shows the importance of drafting the rules carefully to cater for future events. See also para. 2.6.

1.14 The number and extent of the Rules will depend on the size of the club. A club with a small membership will clearly need a less comprehensive set of Rules than a club with, say, 2000 members. Any rules should deal with the following matters:

- the name of the club;
- the purposes and objects of the club;
- membership – admission to membership, discipline of members, resignation and expulsion of members;
- payment of subscriptions;
- management of the club meetings;
- changes and amendments to the rules; and
- dissolution of the club.

1.15 A large club will need a more comprehensive set of rules than a small club, particularly if it has a disciplinary function. All the matters mentioned in the previous paragraph will need more detailed attention. For example, the club may wish to have a Patron, a President, and Vice-presidents. If it leases or owns property, it will need to have Trustees: see paras. 1.51 to 1.54 below. It may also need to make more detailed provisions relating to membership, the management of the club, financial matters, and the power to make byelaws or regulations.

1.16 Some clubs – for example, the Football Association, Rotary, the Round Table and the Women's Institute, to name but a few – are umbrella organisations which have a large number of local clubs under their jurisdiction. These local clubs may be affiliated to the umbrella organisation. In some cases, the affiliated club may be subject to a considerable degree of control. The umbrella organisation may, for example, require the affiliated club to adopt a standard set of rules approved by it. This is particularly likely to happen with sports clubs where the umbrella organisation is concerned to ensure that all its affiliates observe the same rules for the sport. In other cases, the affiliated clubs may have individual sets of rules with as many different variations as there are clubs. The umbrella organisation may provide sets of model rules to its affiliates but without making observance of the rules mandatory.

In essence, though, whether or not an individual club is subject to the requirements of an umbrella organisation, the fact is that each club is a club in its own right and is subject to the same general principles of club law. There are large numbers of umbrella organisations. They cater for clubs engaged in a very wide range of activities – ranging from football, cricket, fencing and morris-dancing to backgammon, model railways, chess, veteran and vintage cars and tiddly winks. They also include political associations, arts societies and allotment association. The list is long.

1.17 The rules of the club are the express terms of the members' contract of membership, as we have seen. In the law of contract, there is a rule that a term may be implied into the contract if there is no express term dealing with a particular matter. The reason for implying a rule is to fill a gap in the express rules, but this is only possible if:

1. the express terms do not deal with the issue which has arisen; and
2. it can be argued that there is room to imply a term.

In the case of a club, this means that – in addition to the express rules – it is possible for rules to be implied but any implied rules will be limited in their scope. If a rule of wider application is felt to be necessary, the rules should be changed. This is done by proposing amendments to them at a general meeting. In para. 1.27 there is a fuller discussion of implied rules. Changes to the rules are discussed at paras. 1.37 to 1.41 below.

The Club's purpose and objects

1.18 The Club's objects should be drafted in such a way as to include all the activities it may wish to pursue. This means, in practice, that the objects should be drafted widely so as to make sure that the Club's funds and assets are spent in a proper manner. Otherwise, the committee would be exposed to accusations that they had incurred expenditure which was outside the rules and thus that they were personally liable for the expenditure. The question of the personal liability of members of the committee is discussed in Chapter 3.

1.19   Much depends on the nature of the club. Sports clubs may wish to encourage one or more sports but also make their premises available to members who do not wish to become involved in the sport. Such a club might then decide to have two main classes of members: sporting members and social members. On the other hand, a club established for non-sporting purposes – for example, the encouragement of card games – might wish to limit its objects to the playing of those games. But it would be sensible for it to make sure that its objects rule would cater for future changes. To do so, the objects rule would need to be widely drafted.

1.20   An example of this type of problem is a case which involved the Hurlingham Club, *Thellusson v Viscount Valentia* (1907). The Club's objects stated that the Club was set up "for the purpose of providing a ground for pigeon-shooting, polo, and other sports". In 1905, a majority of members passed a resolution discontinuing pigeon-shooting at the club. A minority of members brought an action against the Club asking the Court to rule that the resolution was null and void on the grounds that pigeon-shooting was a primary purpose of the club. The Club argued that its fundamental purpose was the association of members for sporting purposes. It won. The Court decided that the rule change was valid. See also para. 1.36 below, where rule changes are looked at.

1.21   Another example is *Baker v Jones* (1954). Payments were made by the British Amateur Weightlifters' Association to solicitors to defend libel actions against some of its members. These were held to be illegal since there was no power in the Rules to use the funds in this way. If the rules had contained a rule allowing the funds to be used in that way, then the outcome of the case would have been completely different. This shows the importance of the drafting of the rules.

1.22   In the light of possible problems of the sort outlined above, the objects rule of the club should set out its main object(s). A sports club, for example, might wish to have two main classes of members: sporting members and social members. In that case, the objects rule should state that its objects are to promote the pursuit of *both* sporting activities *and* social activities. They might go on, for example, to set out as further objects:

- to promote fellowship amongst the members; and
- to foster links with, and to support and co-operate with, organisations with similar objects.

It is common to add a final clause along the following lines: "to do all things necessary for or incidental to or conducive to the attainment of the above-mentioned objects." This gives the club flexibility in its operations.

The following additional rules might also be added at this point:

- a rule listing the sports with which the club is involved; and
- a rule stating that the rules of the sports carried on by the club are the rules adopted by the governing body of the sport in question.

1.23 In the case of a club established to encourage the playing of card games (see example above), the objects rule should specify the card games to be encouraged. But it would also need to cover future contingencies. A specimen rule might be along these lines:

"The objects of the club shall be:
(1) to encourage and promote the playing of card games;
(2) to provide amenities for the members of the club for the pursuit of such games;
(3) to provide social amenities for the members;
(4) to foster links with other clubs or organisations which have similar objects to those of the club;
(5) to do all things necessary for or incidental to or conducive to the attainment of the above objects."

A separate rule would define the card games to be played. Here too, though, it would be sensible to add a clause along the lines of "and such other games as the Committee may from time to time consider to be appropriate". That would enable other games such as board games (for example, backgammon) to be added if it were thought desirable to do so.

1.24 The main point to be borne in mind by those setting up a club and drafting its rules is that the aim of the objects rule should be to cater for events as yet unforeseen. The Hurlingham Club case is a good example of this.

Implied (non-Express) Rules

1.25 A general rule of the law of contract is that terms may be implied into the contract if there are no express terms dealing with the matter. There are two bases upon which the courts usually imply terms into a contract:

1.   to give business efficacy to the contract; and
2.   to give effect to the obvious but unexpressed intention of the parties.

An example of a rule which might be implied is a rule relating to the behaviour of members. It is likely that the rules would say something *expressly* about the behaviour of members on the Club's premises. If they did not, then a rule would be *implied* to the effect that members should conduct themselves in a proper and suitable manner.

Byelaws and regulations

1.26 As mentioned earlier, a Club's rules may allow for the use of byelaws or regulations. These are appropriate for the detailed regulation of the management and administration of the Club and are exercisable by the managing committee. They allow the committee to proceed without having to obtain the members' agreement at a general meeting. To allow for their use, the Club's rules should contain a power to make byelaws or regulations and give that power to the managing committee. It provides for a more streamlined way of dealing with the administration of the Club and avoids the need for a general meeting of the members to deal with day-to-day matters. The enabling rule should state the purpose(s) for which the byelaws may be made and the byelaws introduced should be consistent with the Club's main rules. They should also not encroach upon the function of the Club's main rules. To avoid arguments that they have not been brought sufficiently to the attention of the members, they should be posted on a noticeboard on the Club's premises.

1.27 An example of an enabling rule might be:

"The Committee may from time to time make and alter Regulations (consistent with these Rules) as it shall think necessary for the well-being of the Club."

The Regulations might, for example, place limits on the number of guests a member may entertain at any time in the Club, or they might set out the Club's dress code. They might also, if the Club serves refreshments and meals, set out the times at which these are available. If a member challenged the introduction of a particular new Regulation, then the challenge would have to be on the grounds that the Regulation was either inconsistent with the Club's Rules and/or that it could not be interpreted as being for the well-being of the Club. Questions relating to interpretation of the Rules are dealt with at para. 1.42.

1.28 There is no right way of dealing with the contents of the byelaws/regulations. It is a matter for the club. So, as mentioned earlier, one club may prefer to set its annual subscription at an extraordinary General Meeting called for the purpose; another club may give power to the committee to set the annual subscription by means of amendments to the byelaws. The first may prefer to go through the formalities of an EGM, the second to use the flexibility of byelaws. It is really a question of how the club wishes to manage its affairs.

Provision for future events

1.29 Over time changes inevitably occur in the nature of the Club and its membership. As we saw in the Hurlingham Club case, *Thellusson v Viscount Valentia* (1907), a Club which starts out to further a particular sport (in that case, pigeon-shooting) may find that that particular sport has declined in popularity. In the case in question, the dispute arose because of a decision to stop pigeon-shooting. The Club's objects stated that the Club was set up "for the purpose of providing a ground for pigeon-shooting, polo, and other sports". The Club argued that its fundamental purpose was the association of members for sporting purposes. The Court accepted the Club's argument.

1.30 The Club's Rules – whether as originally drafted or as later amended – clearly need to cater for future events, so far as it is possible to do so. This means that they need to contain a certain degree of flexibility so that the Club is able to adapt to changing circumstances. In cases where there is a dispute, such as the Hurlingham Club case, two questions need to be asked:

1. Does the rule as drafted cover the current situation?
2. Can it be interpretated in a way that it will cover the events which have happened?

If the rules, as drafted, cannot be interpreted so as to deal with the events which have occurred, then steps will have to be taken to change them. In the case mentioned, the Court's decision meant that the rule was wide enough to deal with the change in sporting activities.

1.31 An example was given in para. 1.13, above, of a sporting club with valuable property which is ripe for re-development. If a majority of members decided to realise the development potential of the land by selling to property developers, the sporting objects of the club would be defeated. Assuming that the club has two main classes of members – playing members and social members – the rules need to make sure that this does not happen. This may be done by (1) limiting the number of social members and (2) disabling them from voting on a motion which would have the effect of defeating the club's main purpose.

1.32 Although it is not possible to cater for all eventualities, clearly it is important that those setting up a club give some thought to future events when they are drafting the rules. The rules should include a rule giving the club power to change its rules: see para. 1.34 below. This raises the question of the position of a member who objects to a rule change.

1.33   In *Doyle v White City Stadium* (1935), the judge gave the example of a club connected with boxing turning itself into a club for conducting horse-racing. If an amendment to the rules giving effect to this change is passed by an appropriate majority of members at a duly constituted meeting, then what is the position of dissenting members? They can either choose to resign or remain a member. If they choose to remain, they will be taken to have acquiesced in the rule change and the change will bind them. Payment of their next subscription would be conclusive of this decision. It is not possible in these circumstances for a member to remain a member but to try to assert that he or she is not bound by the rules change. A further point to note is that members cannot query the validity of a newly introduced rule on the grounds that either it has not come to their attention or that they have not received notice of it. To avoid this sort of argument, the rules should deal with matters relating to communication. See para 2.44 which sets out a specimen rule relating to club communications.

Changing the Rules

1.34   A well-drafted set of Rules should contain a rule enabling the club to change its rules. The absence of a rule would mean that the club without a dissolution rule would not have the power to dissolve itself since it would not have the power to change its rules to include such a rule. The serious consequences of such an omission in the rules need not be gone into here.

1.35   The reason for a rule of this sort arises from the contractual nature of a member's relationship with the other members. It is a basic principle of contract law that a contract can only be varied by the agreement of all the parties to it. In the case of a club, that means that the rules may only be varied by the entire membership. In practice, this means that:

- there should be a rule allowing the rules to be changed; and

- the rules should contain an appropriate procedure for going about rule changes.

The Courts will not imply into the rules a power to change them. There needs to be an *express* power.

1.36 An example of the problems which may arise is the case of *Harington v Sendall* (1903). A member of the Oxford and Cambridge University Club agreed to be bound by "the following rules and regulations". The rules did not include a power to change the rules or increase members' subscriptions. The Club wished to increase the members' subscriptions and the member, Mr Harington, objected. The Court upheld his objection. The club argued that:

(a) it had an implied power to change the rules; and
(b) Mr Harington had acquiesced in the rule change because he had not objected to other rule changes.

The Court rejected these arguments and decided that Mr Harington was not bound by the rule change. This decision shows that a different wording of the rule would have stymied Mr Harington's objection. Had the rule stated that he was bound by "such rules and regulations as may be made from time to time", he would have not been able to raise a valid objection.

1.37 The rule enabling changes in the rules should set out an appropriate procedure for changing them. Since a change to the rules affects the entire membership, it is sensible to stipulate that such a change should be the subject of a special meeting called for that specific purpose, usually an Extraordinary General Meeting (EGM). The rules should deal with the following matters:

- the notice requirements for a proposal to change the rules;
- the requirements relating to the draft resolution proposing the change; and
- the nature and size of the majority required for the change to be effective.

If the rule did not stipulate for the size of the majority required, a resolution to change the rules could be valid if passed by a simple majority. The absence of a stipulated two-thirds majority would then enable changes affecting the membership at large to be passed without substantial support of the members being shown.

1.38 So, the following questions need to be considered:

- Who may call the EGM – the committee alone or a group of members?
- If a group of members, how many?
- How much notice of the meeting should be given?
- How much notice of any resolution(s) should be given?
- How many signatures are required for a motion proposed by members?
- What majority is required a for a resolution for a rule change?

1.39 A rule allowing rule changes might be drafted as follows:

1. *"The General Committee may call an extraordinary general meeting of the Club on giving twenty-one days' notice to members which shall include notice of any motion to be discussed by the meeting.*

2. *The General Committee shall also call an extraordinary general meeting on the written requisition of [number] members with the power to vote on giving notice as above, to consider solely any motion specified in the requisition.*

3. *Notice of any motion to be proposed at an extraordinary general meeting must be given as part of the notice by which the meeting is called.*

4. *In the case of a motion for a new rule or alteration of a rule, the motion shall be deemed not to have been carried unless –*
   a. *at least fifty members with the power to vote are present, and*
   b. *the members voting in favour of the motion are not less than forty and comprise not less than two-thirds of the members with the power to vote present and voting."*

For further discussion of meetings, see paras. 3.102 to 3.145.

1.40 Here too it is important to be aware of the interpretation of the rules. A rule stating that the Annual General Meeting is to be used "for general purposes" does not give a power to amend the rules of the Club: see *Harington v Sendall* (above).

1.41 Finally, what is the position of members who object to changes in the rules? They may try to argue that the change was not covered by the rules, for example because the rule change is inconsistent with the club's purpose and objects (as in the Hurlingham Club case) or because the change was not permitted by the rules (as in the Oxford and Cambridge Club case). If those arguments fail or are not available, then the members who object have an election, as it is called. They have the choice ("election") of resigning or of continuing as members. In the second case, their continued membership of the club and, particularly, the payment of a subscription instalment, will mean that they will be taken to have affirmed the new rule. What they cannot do is continue as members and claim not to be bound by the rules.

Interpretation of the Rules

1.42 It should be clear from what has been said above that interpretation is an important aspect of dealing with a club's rules. In other words, the question which often arises is: "What does this particular rule mean?" That is what interpretation is about. (Another word which is sometimes used in this context is "construction".)

1.43 As we have seen, the rules contain the terms of the contract which the members of the club have entered into with each other. There are rules for interpreting contracts, but in recent years the courts have made it clear that club rules may be interpreted differently from ordinary contracts. In *Re GKN Nuts& Bolts Ltd Sports and Social Club* (1982), the Judge said:

> "[T]here is a considerable degree of informality in the conduct of the affairs of such clubs, and ... the courts have to be ready to allow general concepts of reasonableness, fairness and common sense to be given more than their usual weight when confronted by claims to the

contrary which appear to be based on any strict interpretation and rigid application of the letter of the rules. In other words, allowance must be made for some play in the joints."

The judge did emphasise, though, that "scrupulous observance of the rules" is needed when it comes to changing the property rights of members. The same would apply to the interpretation of rules dealing with the suspension or expulsion of a member. As can be seen from some of the cases quoted above, the rules need to be construed or interpreted in the context of the Club's objects clause. Hence its importance.

1.44 It is possible to have a rule which gives the committee power to rule on the interpretation of a particular rule in the event of a dispute. But, in the event of a dispute involving the rules of a club, the Court has the role of interpreting the rules and adjudicating on any disputes. That jurisdiction cannot be removed. It is not, therefore, permissible for a rule to give the committee the final say in interpreting the rules because this would be an ouster of the court's jurisdiction and so would be void. It is sensible for the rules to make provision for the resolution of internal disputes: see para. 1.48, below.

Breach of the rules by a member

1.45 A member of a club has a contractual relationship with all the other members of the club. If he or she breaks one of the club's rules that amounts to a breach of contract. This is because the club's rules contain the terms of the contract. A breach of the rules is, therefore, a breach of contract.

1.46 In view of this, it is sensible to have a rule which expressly states that all members are bound by and must comply with the rules and (if there are any) regulations of the club. They may also say something like:

"No member shall conduct himself or herself within the Clubhouse in a manner which constitutes conduct unbefitting a member of the Club

or, whether within or outside the Clubhouse, in a way which brings or is calculated to bring the Club into disrepute."

Clearly, a rule such as this is likely to give rise to problems of interpretation. Note that the draft above includes the phrases "conduct unbefitting a member of the club", "whether within or outside the Clubhouse" and "brings or is calculated to bring the Club into disrepute". All these phrases are open to interpretation.

1.47 Breaches of the rules may take a variety of different forms and may be minor or serious. They may range from unbecoming conduct on the club's premises to failure to pay the membership subscription. They may also take place on a single occasion or be regular or persistent. The rules therefore need to be flexible and cater for the different outcomes which may follow from breaches of them. This includes putting in place an appropriate procedure for investigating any breach and providing for an appropriate sanction. This is important and is dealt with in Chapter 2: see paras. 2.90 to 2.119.

Internal disputes

1.48 Inevitably, disagreements arise in a club. Several of the cases mentioned in the text arose from disagreements. In the absence of an internal resolution of the disagreements, some of the members resorted to litigation. Examples are *Thellusson v Viscount Valentia* (involving the Hurlingham Club), *Baker v Jones* (involving the British Amateur Weightlifters' Association) and *Harington v Sendall* (involving the Oxford and Cambridge Club). On the whole, clubs prefer to avoid the publicity which litigation involves. Those drafting the rules should therefore make provision for private dispute resolution. This will usually involve mediation or arbitration. This matter is discussed more fully in Chapter 2, at para. 2.125.

Ownership of the Club's property

1.49 Some clubs do not need premises to conduct their activities. Others do. Clearly, a sporting club needs premises for its activities. On the other hand, a club such as a reading group or sewing circle does not need premises to operate.

1.50 The term "the Club's property" covers the premises and land on which the club operates. But it also includes what is called "personal property". This is property other than land, such as paintings, furniture and the like. This section deals with both types of property.

1.51 Since, as we have seen, a club has no legal personality – unlike a company – it cannot hold property in its own name. Named individuals must hold the property (whether it is freehold or held under a lease) on behalf of the members. Clearly, it would be impossible for the entire membership to be named as owners of the land or grantees of the lease. So, the law makes provision for a small number of persons to be registered as owners or named as grantees of the lease. They are called trustees, since they hold the property on trust for the members of the club. If the property is freehold, the relevant deed will name the trustees as transferees of the property. If the property is leasehold (that is, held under a lease), the grantees of the lease will be the trustees, who, again, hold the lease on trust for the members. The trustees' obligations are governed by the law of Trusts.

1.52 The nature of the trust in this context is what is called a 'bare' trust. This type of trust arises where the trustee holds the property for an adult beneficiary absolutely. In the case of a club, the trustees hold the property on trust for the members of the club (who are the beneficiaries under the trust), in accordance with the rules of the club and under the direction of the committee. The trustees' control over the property is limited and they are not obliged to carry out any active duties as trustees. They hold the legal title of the club's property and are subject to the direction of the beneficiaries (the members of the club) acting through the committee. The existence of the trustees is to do with the need for the property to be put in the name of a small number of named persons. It has no bearing on the contractual relationship between the members of the club. Effectively, the trustees remain in the background and need have no involvement in the management of the club.

1.53 Despite this, the club's rules should make provision for the trustees. They will need to deal with the following matters:

- appointment, retirement and removal of the trustees
- the relationship of the trustees with the club
- whether the trustees may participate in the running of the club
- whether they are entitled to attend committee meetings
- if they are entitled to attend, whether they may
  - ○ actively participate in the conduct of the meetings and
  - ○ whether they may take part in a vote.

There is no obligation on the club to include the trustees in the running of the club. The point is that the rules need to be clear about their role. If the rules do not specify a role for them, then they would not be entitled to attend committee meetings or be involved in the management of the club. See para. 3.5 for a fuller discussion.

1.54 A further point to note is that, if the trustees were to be involved in the business of the Club's committee, they would be exposed to the risk of liability in the same way as members of the committee: see para. 3.51. For this reason, it is best that they should remain in the background.

Dissolution of the Club

1.55 The founding members of a club are unlikely to turn their minds to the possibility of it coming to an end. Yet, when drawing up the rules of the club, they should consider the possibility that, for whatever reason, it may be necessary to put an end to it. The cases provide many examples of clubs or societies established for purposes which, at the time of their foundation, were fashionable or popular. As time passes, the once-numerous membership dwindles until only a handful of members remain. At this point, the question arises as to whether the club can still be said to be in existence and what should be done with its assets. This question does not only arise, though, in relation to clubs which run into problems because of lack of money or a dwindling membership. The rules should cater for the possibility that the club may come to end when it is still fully solvent and should set out what should happen to the club's property.

1.56 This means that one of the rules of the new club should relate to its dissolution. This rule should deal with two matters:

1. in what circumstances and by what means it may be dissolved; and
2. on its dissolution how its assets should be distributed.

In the absence of a dissolution rule, those left to deal with the dissolution will be confronted with difficult problems. These can be avoided if there is a suitable dissolution rule in place.

1.57 The case of *Hanchett-Stamford v Attorney General* (2008) provides a good example of this type of problem. It related to an association called 'The Performing and Captive Animals Defence League', which was founded in 1914. The League was an unincorporated association. In other words, its structure was that of a club. In 1962, the League had some 250 members, but, by the late 1970s, it was much less active. Mr and Mrs Hanchett-Stamford joined as life members in the mid-1960s. Eventually, by the late 1990s, the only members left were the Hanchett-Stamfords; the League owned a substantial property which, by the time the case came on, was valued at £1.77 million. Mr Hanchett-Stamford died in 2006. The question now arose as to what to do with the property. Bearing in mind that an association needs to have at least two members to be capable of being an association, on Mr Hanchett-Stamford's death the association effectively ceased to exist. The purpose of Mrs Hanchett-Stamford's case was to ask the court to decide who owned the property. It is clear from the case that a great deal of material relating to the League, particularly the rules drawn up when it was founded, was missing. The only information the court had was a booklet produced in 1962. The court concluded that Mrs Hanchett-Stamford owned the property outright.

1.58 The conclusion reached by the judge may appear surprising, and was undoubtedly not what would have been desired by the founding members in 1914. The problem was that there was scanty information to go on. The significance of this case is that it shows the importance of catering for what may appear to the founding members of a club to be an unwelcome possibility. But that possibility must be dealt with from the outset, so as to avoid the problems which may otherwise arise.

1.59 The rule relating to dissolution should deal with the following matters:

1. what events may trigger dissolution;
2. the procedure to be followed for the members to dissolve the club; and
3. how the assets available upon dissolution are to be distributed.

1.60 A decision to dissolve the club will require a motion of the members and a special meeting. Because of the nature of the situation, the rules should stipulate the following requirements:

- a motion to dissolve the club;
- a meeting specially convened for the purpose of considering that motion;
- the number of members needed to sign the requisition for the meeting;
- how many days' notice of the meeting should be given; and
- the size of majority needed to pass the motion.

For such an event, the majority would be either two thirds or three quarters of those present at the meeting and entitled to vote. The topic of meetings is discussed in Chapter 3, at para. 3.102.

1.61 The rules should also deal with the distribution of the assets of the club on dissolution. In the light of what has been said above, they should say something. Otherwise, it is likely that the matter will end up having to be resolved by a court. So, for example, the rules might say:

"If on dissolution of the Club a surplus shall arise, it shall be distributed equally between all ordinary and overseas members whose subscription is not in arrear at the time of such distribution."

It is up to those drafting the dissolution rule to decide what to do with the club's assets. One solution is to allow the remaining members to share in the club's assets, as seen in the specimen rule above. But that is not necessary. It is perfectly permissible for the rules to stipulate that the remaining assets should be applied elsewhere, for example to a neighbouring club with similar objects.

2. The Club and its Members

Introduction

2.1 This chapter deals with the club's relationship with its members. It looks at the following matters:

- admission to membership;
- treatment of members;
- discipline of members and termination of membership; and
- resolution of disputes.

2.2 The Equality Act 2010 is important here. It particularly affects the treatment of candidates to membership and the treatment of members. Single-sex clubs have been a source of discussion at the time of writing; the relevant provisions of the Act are looked at. Equality law also affects clubs in other respects, however. For example, a complaint may be made against a club on the grounds that it has discriminated against a member of its staff or a contractor doing work on the club's premises. These aspects are important but are not relevant to this chapter. They are discussed in Chapter 4: see paras. 4.77 to 4.92.

2.3 The second section of the chapter deals with the treatment of members in three ways:

1. communications between the club and the members;
2. data protection; and
3. the impact of the Equality Act on the club's treatment of its members.

2.4 The third section deals with the treatment of members under the rules. The focus is on the discipline of members who break the rules and the procedures the club should follow in dealing with them. is examined in the context of the rules. In view of the paramount importance of the rules, those responsible for dealing with members who breach the rules (usually the Committee) need to ensure that their actions and the actions of anyone else involved comply with the Rules. This is particularly important when it comes to termination of membership. The section ends with a discussion of the resignation of members.

2.5 The final section deals with the resolution of internal disputes. It is not possible to oust the jurisdiction of the courts. It is possible, though, to provide machinery for resolving the disputes without going to court – by means of mediation and/or arbitration.

Categories of membership

Introduction

2.6 Most clubs have different categories of membership; this is more likely in the case of a larger club. The rules should identify clearly the different categories of membership available and set out the rights and obligations of each category of members. Most of the members are likely to be "ordinary" or "full" members. Depending on the size and nature of the club, the rules may also make provision for the following classes of members:

- ordinary members
- social members
- overseas members
- temporary members
- associate members
- junior members
- honorary members
- life members.

The rules should specify the nature of each type of membership and what it entails. Again, depending on the nature of the club, the rules need to set out any qualifications needed for a particular category of membership. In Chapter 1 an example was given of a sports club with two categories of members: ordinary playing members and non-playing social members. If, for example, the club were to receive an offer from a property developer to buy the club's land at a good price, there would be the risk that the social members would outvote the playing members and vote for a sale. That would defeat the club's objects. The rules therefore should address such a possibility. One way to do so is to give different voting rights to each of the two categories so that the social members are unable to vote for a motion put to a general meeting which would be potentially prejudicial to the interests of the playing members. That would prevent the social members from forcing a sale against the wishes of the playing members.

2.7 In the case of a sports club, the rules might specify a certain level of playing ability, for example that playing members should have at least a certain golfing handicap.

2.8 Joining a club may involve a selection process, which again may vary according to the different categories of membership and the size of the club. In some cases, the rules may stipulate that membership is by invitation only; in others, they may set out a more elaborate process. It is normal for the selection process to be delegated to the club's committee, since a requirement for the process to be undertaken by the members in general meeting, for example, would be cumbersome. So, the rules may stipulate that a candidate should be proposed and seconded by existing members to whom the candidate is known. They may also require that applications are considered by the committee and that, as a pre-requisite to consideration, candidates should be interviewed by a member of the committee. If the club has a candidates' book, the rules may require that candidates should be supported by a stipulated number of members before their candidature is considered by the committee. The term often used in relation to becoming a member of a club is that the candidate has been "elected" to membership, the process being called "election". Again, this is more likely if the club is large.

2.9 Most of the members of the club are likely to be "full" or "ordinary" members. This category of members will have the fullest range of rights and privileges. The other categories are likely to be given a more restricted range of entitlements.

2.10 The club should consider what range of entitlements to give each category of members. Relevant considerations are:

- limits on numbers in each category;
- qualifications for each category, for example a minimum handicap in the case of a golf club;
- definition of the category, for example what is meant by "temporary" and "overseas";
- restrictions on usage of the club applicable to categories of member other than ordinary members;
- voting restrictions in relation to motions at general meetings; and
- eligibility to stand for election to the committee or to be an officer of the club

Full or ordinary members

2.11 Full or ordinary members are members who pay an entrance fee on joining the club (if any is payable under the rules) and then pay an annual subscription. They are thus annual members in the sense that they pay their subscription on a yearly basis, even if it is paid in monthly, quarterly or half-yearly instalments. It would be open to a club to offer longer-term membership (for example, for 2, 3 or 5 years) if it wished to raise a larger sum of money in the short term.

Social members

2.12 This category of members would exist in a sports club, for example. The rules need to set a limit on the numbers eligible for election to this category and what restrictions should be set on their ability to vote for motions at general meetings.

Overseas members

2.13 Overseas members are, by definition, those who live outside the United Kingdom. Due to their status, they may be required to pay a lower subscription than full members. To avoid any arguments, the rules should define the term "overseas". They may also stipulate that overseas members may spend up to a specified number of nights in the club (if it is a residential club) during any calendar year, but that, if they spend in excess of the specified number, they will become liable for a full subscription rather than a reduced subscription. The rules should also deal with the selection process, which may be the same as for the selection of full members.

Temporary members

2.14 Temporary members are, as the name implies, those who are members for a limited time only. The rules need to deal specifically with this category. The following matters should be addressed:

- the process of admission, for example on the authority of a specified number of committee members;
- the duration of the membership; and
- any restrictions on their use of the club facilities.

Associate members

2.15 Associate membership has a number of different meanings. It may mean that it is a type of membership which has fewer privileges than full membership and/or that it is a category of membership which a candidate is required to occupy before proceeding to full membership. It may also be a type of membership offered to members of other clubs who are admitted to membership on a temporary basis, for example, because their own club is closed for meals at the weekend. If the club decides to have such a category of membership, then the rules need to deal with the matter. It should be noted that the Equality Act 2010 applies to "associates", as defined by section 107(6): see para. 4.90, below.

Junior members

2.16 Junior membership may be appropriate in certain types of club, particularly sports clubs. The term "junior" implies a person under the age of 18. Those under 18 are known in law as "minors" and have limited capacity to enter into contracts. For example, a minor would not be liable to pay his or her annual subscription. For this reason, the rules should make clear what privileges or restrictions apply to this category. They may also make provision for the minor to apply to become a full member on attaining the age of majority.

2.17 It should also be noted that the Equality Act 2010 may affect the treatment given by a club to its different categories of members: see paras. 2.71, below.

Honorary members

2.18 Honorary membership of the club may be given to members or non-members of the club. In the case of members, it may be given as a reward for past services to the club. In the case of non-members it may be offered to those who are eminent in a particular field and whose membership of the club would enhance its standing or be of assistance to it in some way. Honorary members usually do not pay any entrance fee or annual subscription. The rules should provide for the election of such members and should deal with matters such as:

1. the number of such members who may be elected in any one year;
2. the method of election – for example, whether the committee should be unanimous when electing them;
3. whether they may propose or second candidates for membership;
4. whether they have any voting rights at meetings; and
5. whether they are eligible for election to any office within the club.

In the last two cases, it is normal for honorary members to be ineligible to vote and ineligible for election to any office. The rules may also prevent them from participating in any surplus of funds on the dissolution of the club.

Life members

2.19 Life membership of the club means, as its name implies, that a member is a member of the club for life. This category of membership may be available to members who pay their subscription in one lump sum, discounted for the fact that the club is receiving most of the money in advance of when it would otherwise have become payable. Life members normally enjoy the same privileges of membership, except for the fact that an annual subscription is no longer payable. Sometimes, clubs create a category of *honorary* life membership for members who have given long service to the club and from whom no further subscription is expected. If the club has such a category of membership, the rules should deal with matters such as:

1. the resignation or expulsion of the life member; and
2. the power of the club to ask for an additional levy from life members in the event of it needing to raise money to cover an unexpected expense.

If there is no such provision, the club would not be able to ask a life member to pay an additional levy.

Admission to membership

2.20 *In theory*, it is open to a club to refuse membership to anyone who it – or its membership committee – decides does not fit in with its ethos or purposes. This is based on the idea of freedom of contract. The theory is that it is open to a person to choose or not to choose to enter into a contract with someone else. Since the relations of the members of the club are governed by a contract, it follows that they may choose not to admit someone to their ranks.

2.21 The enactment of legislation regarding equality means that this idea of freedom of contract should be treated with care. There have been Acts dealing with race and sex discrimination since the 1970s and later legislation dealing with other forms of discrimination. The effect of this legislation has been to qualify the traditional idea of freedom of contract. It has now been consolidated into the Equality Act 2010. Clubs are affected by its provisions.

2.22 The first part of this section will explain generally the main features of the legislation. The second part will explain how they apply to clubs: see paras. 2.32 to 2.37.

General provisions of the Equality Act 2010

2.23 Generally speaking, an act of unlawful discrimination takes place where the alleged victim is treated in a way which the Act identifies as unlawful and that treatment is on the grounds of what it calls "protected characteristics". Two matters need to be considered here:

1. what the "protected characteristics" are; and
2. what amounts to unlawful discrimination.

Protected Characteristics

2.24 Sections 4 – 12 of the Act set out the list of "protected characteristics". These include:

- age
- disability
- gender reassignment
- marriage and civil partnership
- pregnancy and maternity
- race
- religion or belief
- sex
- sexual orientation.

"Race" includes ethnic or national origin, colour and nationality.

Unlawful discrimination

2.25 The following types of discrimination are made unlawful by the Act:

- direct discrimination (section 13)
- indirect discrimination (section 19)
- harassment (section 26)
- victimisation (section 27)

Specific examples of how the Act may affect clubs are given later: see paras. 2.74, 2.76, 2.77 and 2.78.

2.26 *Direct discrimination* occurs where a person (A) treats another person (B) less favourably because:

1. B has a protected characteristic; or
2. A *thinks* that B has a protected characteristic; or
3. B *is connected with* someone with that protected characteristic.

An obvious example of the first type of direct discrimination is where A treats B less favourably because she is a woman. The second type of discrimination is known as discrimination by perception. The third type is known as discrimination by association or associative discrimination. This type of discrimination occurs when a person is discriminated against not because they have the protected characteristic but because they are associated with someone who does. For examples, see para. 2.74 below. In all three cases B's circumstances must be similar enough to the circumstances of the person being treated more favourably for a valid comparison to be made.

2.27 The Act states that an act of direct discrimination takes place where A treats B less favourably *because of* a protected characteristic. In other words, the reason for the less favourable treatment must be the protected characteristic. This means that if A treats B less favourably for a reason which has nothing to do with a protected characteristic, there will not be an unlawful act of direct discrimination. For example, A demotes B (who has a protected characteristic) because of B's incompetence. The protected characteristic is not the reason for the demotion. A would commit an unlawful act of direct discrimination against B, though, if it was established that someone without the protected characteristic would have been treated differently and not demoted. The definition of direct discrimination implies an inequality of treatment between two people where the inequality arises because of the difference in treatment and the reason for the difference is that one of them has a protected characteristic.

2.28 *Indirect discrimination* takes place when there is a "provision, criterion or practice" (PCP) that applies in the same way for everybody but disadvantages a group of people who share a protected characteristic, and the alleged victim is disadvantaged as part of this group. If this happens, the person or organisation applying the provision, criterion or practice must show that there is a good reason for it. The phrase "provision, criterion or practice" is wide and includes a policy, practice, rule or arrangement. In effect, it means doing something to a member which has (or would have) a worse impact on them than on people who do not share that characteristic. It makes no difference that there was no intention to disadvantage anyone.

2.29 A person claiming to be the victim of indirect discrimination must establish the following:

- there is a provision, criterion or practice which an organisation is applying equally to everyone (or to everyone in a group that includes the claimant);
- the provision, criterion or practice disadvantages people with the claimant's protected characteristic when compared with people without it;
- the provision, criterion or practice has disadvantaged the claimant personally or that it will disadvantage them; and
- the organisation cannot show that the provision, criterion or practice is a "proportionate means of achieving a legitimate aim".

This last requirement means that there must be a good reason for applying the provision, criterion or practice despite the level of disadvantage to people with the claimant's protected characteristic. If the organisation can show there is a good reason for its policy, there is no indirect discrimination. For examples, see para. 2.41 below.

2.30 *Harassment* takes place where a person is treated in a way that violates their dignity, or creates a hostile, degrading, humiliating or offensive environment. For example, a man with Down's syndrome is visiting a pub with friends. The bar staff make derogatory and offensive comments about him, which upset and offend him.

2.31 *Victimisation* occurs when someone is treated unfairly if he or she is taking action under the Equality Act (like making a complaint of discrimination), or if he or she is supporting someone else who is doing so. For example, an employee makes a complaint of racial harassment at work and is dismissed as a consequence.

Application of the Equality Act to clubs

2.32 The Act applies to what it calls "associations". The definition of this term (in section 107) includes clubs which have at least 25 members and admission to which is governed by the association's rules and includes a process of selection. The rules need not be written. Most clubs are likely to be within the definition, unless they have fewer than 25 members. The sorts of groups likely to fall outside the Act are smaller groups or organisations which do not have a selection procedure. Examples are a video club where a person becomes a member in order to hire films or a gym or health club where a person pays a joining fee or monthly subscription to obtain access to the exercise facilities. Even if they have the title 'club' or 'society', they are not within the definition in section 107.

2.33 The definitions of unlawful discrimination considered above (at paras. 2.25 to 2.31) – direct and indirect discrimination, harassment and victimisation – apply to the provisions of the Act dealing with clubs. The three types of direct discrimination mentioned there should also be borne in mind in this context.

2.34 Section 101(1) of the Act makes unlawful the following types of discrimination against applicants for membership:

- discrimination in the arrangements it makes for deciding who to admit to membership;
- discrimination in the terms on which it is prepared to offer membership; and
- discrimination by not accepting a candidate's application for membership.

Clubs for those with shared protected characteristics

2.35 It is possible for a club to restrict its membership to those who share a single protected characteristic. So, a club which restricts its membership to men will not contravene section 101, since it is restricting membership to those with one shared protected characteristic: see Schedule 16, para. 1(1). It should be noted that this paragraph does not apply to colour. This means that a club cannot restrict membership based on skin colour. On the other hand, if a club called the Black Women's Culture Club states that membership is open to any woman whose origins are in Africa or the Caribbean, that would be permissible since membership is based on ethnic origin rather than colour. (This example is taken from the Government Equality Office's Guidance on the application of the Act to private clubs and other associations.

See: www.gov.uk/guidance/equality-act-2010-guidance. The Government Equality Office is now called the Women and Equalities Unit.)

2.36 On the other hand, if the club tries to impose a further restriction, it will contravene the Act. So, a men-only club may not restrict its membership to men of a particular religious persuasion or race since that would be to restrict membership to those with two shared characteristics – sex and religion, or sex and race. Similarly, a gay men's choir would contravene the act by refusing to admit a gay man who was Muslim. (This example is also taken from the Government Equality Office's Guidance on the application of the Act to private clubs and other associations.)

2.37 Similar considerations apply in relation to the other protected characteristics. In relation to disability, for example, it is permissible for a club for deaf people to restrict its membership to those who are deaf or partially deaf. It can refuse membership to those with a different disability.

Direct discrimination

2.38 What has been said so far relates to clubs which impose restrictions on membership. If a club refuses membership from persons or charges them a higher membership fee because, for example, they are Jews or gay Christians, that would amount to direct discrimination on the grounds of race (in the first case) and the combined grounds of religion and sexual orientation (in the second case). So, too, a sports club which has members of both sexes would commit an act of sex discrimination if it laid down different rules of admission relating to practice times, for example, that male members could play at all times, whereas female members could only play at specified times.

2.39 As a general rule it is not possible for someone committing an act of direct discrimination to justify that discrimination. If *age* discrimination is involved, however, it is possible to justify direct discrimination if the person committing the act can show that it is a "proportionate means of achieving a legitimate aim": see section 13(2). The issue of age discrimination may arise in the context of admission to a club, for example if the club sets a minimum age requirement for admission to membership. It is more likely to arise, though, in relation to differentiated rates of subscription for members. This issue is dealt with below, at para. 2.71.

2.40 One type of direct discrimination is discrimination by association: see para. 2.26 above. So, for example, a candidate for membership of a cricket club is refused membership because he or she has a disabled parent, and the membership committee is concerned that, because of the caring responsibilities involved, he or she will not be reliable in turning up for practice sessions and matches. That is an example of unlawful discrimination because of the candidate's association with the disabled parent.

Indirect discrimination

2.41 *Indirect* discrimination was discussed at para. 2.28 above. As we saw there, an act of indirect discrimination will not be unlawful if the person applying the "provision, criterion or practice" (PCP) is able to justify it on the grounds that it is a proportionate means of achieving a legitimate aim. For example, a Jewish cricket player wishes to join the local cricket club which always has its practice days on a Saturday but for that reason does not feel able to apply. That would be likely to be an act of indirect discrimination on the grounds of religion. On the other hand, the club might be able to justify the practice on the grounds that no other day of the week could be found to be satisfactory. Similarly, a rugby club might legitimately exclude all those – including disabled persons – who are incapable of participating in the sport.

Harassment and victimisation

2.42 *Harassment* and *victimisation* are more likely to arise in relation to the treatment of members. Nevertheless, the Act makes specific provision for applicants for membership in relation to both types of discrimination. Section 101(4) states that a club must not harass a candidate for membership of the club. Further, section 101(5) states that a club must not victimise a candidate in one of three ways:

1. in the arrangements it makes for deciding on membership admission;
2. in the terms on which it is prepared to offer membership; and
3. by rejecting the candidate's application.

As an example of victimisation it is appropriate to consider the position of a candidate for membership of a club. It comes to light that the candidate gave evidence in legal proceedings on behalf of a friend who was suing the club. As a result of this information coming to light, the candidate's application is rejected by the membership committee. The rejection of the application is an unlawful act of victimisation falling with sections 27(2) and 101(5)(c).

Treatment of members

2.43 This section deals with three aspects:

1. Communications between the club and the members;
2. Data protection in relation to members; and
3. The impact of the Equality Act 2010 on the treatment of members.

The data protection legislation is important in relation to members' records and how the club deals with them. It is dealt with in the next section. The third section looks at the effect of the Equality Act 2010.

Communications

2.44 The rules should provide for communications between the club and the members. This has two aspects:

1. The members should be required to provide the club with up-to-date information about their personal details, particularly

details relating to their email address, personal address and telephone numbers; and

2. The rules should deal with communications from the club to the membership and, in particular:

    (1) how communication may be made generally;

    (2) how notices of meetings should be communicated; and

    (3) the consequences of non-arrival or late arrival of such notices.

2.45 *Members* Apart from requiring up-to-date personal details, the rules may also require them to specify how they may be contacted. For example, the rules may say that all communications will be by means of email and that any member who wishes to be contacted by post must expressly notify the club in writing to this effect.

2.46 *The Club* The rules should deal with communications generally and also in relation to notices of meetings. They may provide for notices to be posted in writing in the clubhouse and on the club's website. They should also provide for communication both by post and by electronic means. They should make clear the following matters:

- that notices sent to members – by whatever means – will be deemed to have arrived within a certain time after despatch by the club (for example, two days);
- that the non-arrival or late arrival of a notice sent by the club will not invalidate any meeting convened by the club; and
- that the accidental omission to give due notice to one or more members of the club will similarly not invalidate any meeting.

Data protection

2.47 The club must comply with the relevant data protection legislation in relation to the way it deals with its members. The main items of legislation were originally the Data Protection Act 2018 (DPA) and the General Data Protection Regulation 2018 (GDPR). The DPA is a UK Act of Parliament; the Regulation comes from the European Union. However, the legislation has been amended to take account of the fact that the UK is no longer a member of the EU. This section will explain the current law.

2.48 The aim of the legislation – set out in section 2 of the DPA – is to protect individuals in relation to the processing of personal data by requiring personal data to be processed lawfully and fairly and by giving them rights to obtain information about the processing of personal data and to require inaccurate information to be corrected. Personal data is to be processed in accordance with the six data protection principles set out in article 5 of the Regulation.

2.49 The following aspects of the legislation will be looked at:

- the definition of "personal data"
- the requirements for lawful processing of data
- data processing
- members' access to data
- membership lists.

In view of the importance of the data protection legislation, it would be sensible for the club to give thought to putting in place rules to deal with possible problems.

Definition of "personal" data"

2.50 The legislation deals with two types of personal data. First is the general definition set out in article 4(1) of the GDPR. There is also a category called "Special categories of personal data", set out in article 9(1). The general definition of "personal data" is:

"any information relating to an identified or identifiable natural person ("data subject"). An identifiable natural person is one who can be identified, directly or indirectly, in particular by reference to an identifier such as a name, an identification number, location data, an online identifier or to one or more factors specific to the physical, physiological, genetic, mental, economic, cultural or social identity of that natural person".

2.51 The definition of "special categories of personal data" in article 9(1) is:

"personal data revealing racial or ethnic origin, political opinions, religious or philosophical beliefs, or trade union membership, and . . .

genetic data, biometric data for the purpose of uniquely identifying a natural person, data concerning health or data concerning a natural person's sex life or sexual orientation".

Lawful processing of personal data

2.52 Personal data within the first category may be processed lawfully if:

1. the data subject (i.e. the member of the club) has agreed; or
2. the club has a legitimate interest in using or storing the data.

See sections 2 and 4(2) and articles 4(11) and 7 and 6(1)(b) – (d) and (f). Article 6(1)(b) – (d) sets out what interests are legitimate. An example of such an interest would be information relating to a member's offensive behaviour towards another member or to a member of the club's staff.

2.53 The special categories of personal data are protected by stricter rules. The processing of this type of data will be lawful only if the requirements of article 9(2) are satisfied. Broadly speaking, they are:

1. the member must give *explicit* agreement; or
2. the processing is necessary for the purpose of legitimate interests pursued by the club.

An example of the second category would be behaviour of a member towards another member or a member of staff which was a criminal offence. The detailed requirements for this are set out in DPA section 10 and Schedules 1, para. 31 and 9, para. 6 and GDPR article 6(1)(d). If they are not satisfied the processing will be unlawful. The club itself should be a not-for-profit body and should be established for political, philosophical, religious or trade union purposes. Two other conditions to be noted are:

1. the processing must relate solely to the members or to former members of the club or to persons who have regular contact with it in connection with its purposes; and

2. the personal data is not disclosed outside that body without the agreement of the member.

Data processing

2.54 The Act applies to what it calls "the automated or structured processing of personal data": s. 21(1). This is defined in two ways:

1. the processing of personal data wholly or partly by automated means; and
2. the processing otherwise than by automated means of personal data which forms part of a filing system or is intended to form part of a filing system.

Note the definition of "data" in GDPR article 4(1), given at paras. 2.50 and 2.52 above. The term "processing" is wide and includes profiling, a term defined in GDPR, article 4(4).

2.55 It is not clear what is meant by the second part of the definition above. But judicial decisions have indicated that manual records will only fall within the definition if "they are of sufficient sophistication to provide the same or similar ready accessibility as a computerised filing system": see *Durant v Financial Services Authority* (2004). The Judge, Lord Justice Auld, went on to add (at para. 48 of the judgement):

> "*To leave it to the searcher to leaf through files, possibly at great length and cost, and fruitlessly, to see whether it or they contain information relating to the person requesting information and whether that information is data within the Act bears . . . no resemblance to a computerised search. It cannot have been intended by Parliament. . ."*

Although this statement would seem to suggest that a club without any organisation in its files would be outside the definition, there is no doubt that a properly run club should make sure that its records are computerised.

Members' access to data

2.56 A club member has the right to obtain from the "data controller" confirmation as to whether or not personal data concerning him or her being processed. If it is being processed, then he or she has access to the personal data and certain types of information. The information, as set out in the GDPR article 15, is as follows:

- the purposes of the processing
- the categories of personal data concerned
- the recipients or categories of recipient to whom the personal data have been or will be disclosed, in particular recipients in third countries or international organisations
- where possible, the envisaged period for which the personal data will be stored, or, if not possible, the criteria used to determine that period
- the existence of the right to request from the controller rectification or erasure of personal data or restriction of processing of personal data concerning the data subject or to object to such processing
- the right to lodge a complaint with the Information Commissioner
- where the personal data are not collected from the data subject, any available information as to their source
- the existence of automated decision-making, including profiling, and meaningful information about the logic involved, as well as the significance and the envisaged consequences of such processing for the data subject.

In addition, the member must satisfy the following conditions:

- he or she must make a formal request to the "data controller" and
- he or she must pay the appropriate fee.

See DPA, section 12 and GDPR, articles 12 and 15. In relation to a club, the data controller will be the secretary.

2.57 A member has various rights under the legislation, including the right to have the data corrected.

2.58 A situation may arise where the data controller (the club secretary) cannot comply with the member's request without disclosing information relating to a third party who is identifiable from that information. In that case, the secretary does not have to comply with the request unless the third party has agreed or it is reasonable to comply with the request without the third party's agreement. In deciding whether to dispense with agreement, the secretary must take into account any duty of confidentiality owed to the third party. The secretary should give the information if it is possible to give it in a redacted form or by omitting the name or other identifying particulars of the third party. See GDPR, article 6(1).

2.59 In the context of a club, it can be seen how problems of this sort might arise. For example, the club's committee may propose to co-opt a member, but the proposal is opposed by one of the members on the grounds that the candidate is persistently drunk and unpleasant. The proposal is rejected by the committee and the discussion is fully recorded in the committee's minutes (which are available to all members of the club). The rejected candidate knows of the discussion and asks the secretary as data controller for the information about him contained in the minutes. The secretary asks the member who opposed the co-option for his agreement for the information in the minutes to be disclosed, but he refuses. So the secretary should supply a redacted copy of the minutes or a relevant extract from them.

2.60 Cases of this sort pose a number of problems which a club needs to consider:

- whether the minutes of committee meetings should be confidential or should be made available to the membership at large
- how the secretary as data controller should deal with requests of this sort.

Needless to say, if the minutes of committee meetings made available to the membership, the minutes of the committee meeting will have to be carefully worded in cases a member affected by a committee decision makes a data subject request.

Membership lists

2.61 It is usually for a club to compile a list of members for circulation to the membership. When a member joins the club, the club will be given personal details such as his or her name, address and other relevant contact details, for example email address or mobile telephone number. At this stage, two questions arise:

1. Does the club have the right to hold these details? and
2. Do the other members of the club have the right of access to these details?

In relation to the first question, it is clear that on joining the club the new member impliedly agrees to the club holding his or her personal details. In relation to the second question – and bearing in mind the nature of a members' club – the answer should be that the new member does impliedly agree to the other members having his/her contact details. If the members have no means of contacting their fellow-members, they would be unable to contact them if, for example, they wish to convene an Extraordinary General Meeting (EGM) involving a requisition signed by 50 members.

2.62 This is a difficult area and, in the light of leakages of club membership lists to the press in recent years, it is understandable that a club's committee may wish to restrict access to the membership list. The appropriate way to deal with this is by means of a discussion at a general meeting and/or by inserting appropriate rules into the club's constitution. In any event, if a list is circulated to the membership – by whatever means – it should be made clear that its contents are protected by the legislation.

2.63 These days most clubs of any size have websites. Parts of the website – for example, details of the club's membership – will be only available to club members in a part of the website access to which is restricted. Access is usually by means of a username and password. This will be subject to the club's privacy policy which includes compliance with the data protection principles. Nevertheless, similar problems are likely to arise as with membership lists in printed form. Again, it is appropriate to deal with this in the club's rules.

2.64 The other aspect to be considered is lists relating to the membership of the club's committee. The name and details of a committee member are protected in the same way as those of an ordinary member. But, on becoming a member of the committee, it is arguable that the new member impliedly agrees to this data being available to the whole membership. This does not include sensitive personal data which would require the new member's express consent before being released. Again, this is a matter which should be dealt with in the rules. For the definition of "sensitive personal data", see para. 2.51 above.

Treatment of members: Equality Act 2010

2.65 The 2010 Act has a considerable impact on the way the club treats those who are already members of it. That is in addition to its impact on the club's admission processes: see para. 2.32 above. This aspect of the Act is considered in the paragraphs that follow.

2.66 First, however, it should be noted that the Act not only embraces members of the club but that it also embraces other people, particularly those who use the club but who are not full members of it. The main categories of such people are:

1. those who use the club's facilities because they are temporary or associate members; and
2. those who are guests or prospective guests.

This second category may be guests of a full member of the club or guests of temporary or associate members. Those in this category are in effect third parties in relation to whom the club may incur liability. Their position is discussed in Chapter 4.

2.67 This section deals with treatment of club members which is contrary to the 2010 Act. The main provisions of the Act have already been dealt with: see paras. 2.23 to 2.31. Before considering their effect in relation to club members, two matters need to be dealt with:

1. the position of sports clubs; and
2. concessions based on age or length of membership.

These are considered in the next two paragraphs.

Sports clubs

2.68 The Act specifically exempts sport from the relevant provision relating to gender and age discrimination in sport. Section 195(1) exempts participation as a competitor in what it calls "a gender-related activity". This is defined by s. 195(3) as

> *"an activity of a competitive nature in which the physical strength, stamina, or technique of average persons of one sex would put them at a disadvantage compared to average persons of the other sex as competitors in events involving the activity".*

The effect is to allow sports which are confined to adult men and women. So a sports club may organise separate senior male and female races. But separate competitions for boys and girls may not be permitted. This depends on the age and stage of development of the children who are likely to be competitors: see section 195(4). If, for example, the club organises junior races for boys and girls up to the age of 12, there is unlikely to be any real difference in strength and stamina between the boys and girls. So, the exemption would not apply to separate races for each separate group.

2.69 Sports teams may be selected to represent a country, place or area if:

1. the selection process is based on nationality, place of birth or length of residence in a particular area or place; or
2. the aim of the selection process is to comply with the rules of a competition.

See section 195(5) and (6).

2.70 Similarly with restrictions by reference to age. Section 195(7) allows what it calls "participation in an age-banded activity", a phrase defined in section 195(8). Participation by reference to age is possible provided it is necessary to do so:

- to obtain fair competition;
- to ensure the safety of competitors;
- to comply with the rules of a national or international competition; or
- to increase participation in that activity.

If it is not necessary to impose the age limits for one of these four reasons the exception will not apply. If it does apply, it allows, for example:

- selection on the basis of age is possible for national and international tournaments where the rules of the tournament require it;
- under 21's football tournaments; and
- veterans' tennis leagues.

Concessions based on age or length of membership

2.71 Questions of *age* discrimination might arise if a club decides to charge different levels of subscription according to the age of its members. Section 13(2) of the Act makes clear that this is permissible if it is "a proportionate means of achieving a legitimate aim". So, for example, to encourage youngsters to participate in the sport at an early age, the local cricket club sets a lower level of subscription for them than for others. Some clubs also grant reduced subscriptions to older members or members who satisfy a stipulated period of membership. Schedule 16, para. 1A makes it clear that such arrangements do not contravene the Act. So, for example, it will be lawful for a club to charge an annual membership fee of £500 to members below 35, £750 to those between 35 and 65, £250 to those over 65 and £100 to those over 80.

Direct discrimination

2.72 Direct discrimination, as we have seen, arises where a person is treated less favourably than someone else on the grounds of a protected characteristic. It may occur in three situations:

1. Where A treats B less favourably because he/she has a protected characteristic; or
2. Where A *thinks* that B has a protected characteristic ("discrimination by perception"); or
3. Where B *is connected with* someone with that protected characteristic ("associative discrimination").

2.73 The Act sets out four situations in which unlawful discrimination may occur:

1. in the way the club gives the member access to a "benefit, facility or service" or by not giving the member such access;
2. by depriving the member of membership;
3. by varying the member's terms of membership; and
4. by subjecting the member to "any other detriment".

See section 101(2).

2.74 It may help to give some examples here:

1. A female member of a tennis club is not allowed to play at the weekends, whereas male members are allowed to play on every day of the week. That is unlawful sex discrimination against a member of a club.
2. A member of staff in the club's bar thinks that a female member is transsexual and refuses to serve her. That is an example of discrimination by perception.
3. A club is holding its annual dinner. The spouses/partners of members are also invited to the dinner as guests of the club. The partner of one member is black and is not invited because the organisers believe that other members and their guests will object. This is direct associative discrimination on racial grounds. (This example is taken from the EHRC's Guidance. See https://www.equalityhumanrights.com/equality/equality-act-2010/equality-act-2010-guiding-principles-associations.) It should be noted that both the member and the partner would have claims against the club. See para. 4.91 for a discussion of the partner's claim.

Indirect discrimination

2.75 Indirect discrimination takes place where a PCP ("provision, criterion or practice") is applied and it disadvantages a group which shares a protected characteristic: see para. 2.29 for a fuller explanation. The phrase "provision, criterion or practice" is very wide and, as the EHRC Guidance makes clear, it effectively means doing something which has (or would have) a worse impact on the member with the particular protected characteristic(s) than on those who do not share that characteristic. "Doing something" can include making a decision, or applying a rule and/or a way of doing things

2.76 In para. 2.41 above, the example was given of a Jewish cricket player wishing to join the local cricket club which always has its practice days on a Saturday but for that reason does not feel able to apply. Similar considerations would apply to a Jewish member of the club who was affected by a change in the arrangements for practising. Previously, he was able to make the practice day but the change to a Saturday would put him at a disadvantage. That would amount to an act of indirect discrimination and would be unlawful unless the club was able to justify it.

Harassment

2.77 *Harassment* was considered at para. 2.30 above. Harassment of a club member would take place, for example, if a female member of the club overheard the club manager making offensive remarks about her.

Victimisation

2.78 *Victimisation* was considered at para. 2.31 above. The Government Guidance cites an example of two members of a club. One of them makes a complaint against the club of sexual harassment and the other member supports the complaint. As a result, both members of the club are denied access to the club until the outcome of the harassment complaint has been determined.

Discipline and termination of membership

Introduction

2.79 Outside the application of the Equality Act, the issue which falls to be dealt with here is the treatment of members who commit a breach of the club's rules. Breaches of the rules range from minor infringements to misconduct which is so serious as to merit expulsion from the club. The relationship between the member and the club is based on a contract; the terms – that is, the obligations – of the contract are to be found in the rules. The rules need to deal expressly, therefore, with the treatment of members who break them. If they do not do so, the club will not be able to deal with the matter. The only way to cope with the problem is to change the rules with a view to providing for future events. The change cannot apply retrospectively.

2.80 One matter worthy of specific mention here is the payment of a member's dues. These are usually the entrance fee and the annual subscription. Although non-payment of such dues is clearly a breach of the member's contract with the Club, it is better to treat non-payment separately from the other breaches which may trigger the Club's disciplinary procedure. Dealing with non-payment separately avoids the need for invoking the disciplinary procedure which is best confined to matters of a genuinely disciplinary nature. Non-payment of dues is considered below: see para. 2.85.

2.81 Those drawing up the club's rules should set out a procedure for dealing with breaches of the rules by members. The important ingredients of the procedure are dealt with in the next section. The procedure need not be elaborate but should be clear and simple and easily applied. A large club may feel the need for a more elaborate procedure than a small one. But the essential point is that the procedure should be followed. If those responsible for applying the procedure – normally the club's committee – fail to follow it or misinterpret it, there is a risk that in the event of litigation the court will declare the club's action void. This is particularly so when expulsion is involved. See para. 2.109, where some of the relevant cases are looked at.

2.82 It would be usual for the procedure to be contained within the main body of the club's rules, but it would be possible for it to be contained within a separate appendix as a set of regulations. The advantage of doing so is that the procedure can be changed without having to go through a rule-change procedure via a general meeting. The disadvantage is that changes in such a fundamental aspect of membership of the club would not be within the control of the members in general meeting. For this reason, it is advisable to retain the procedure within the main body of the rules.

2.83 The procedure should also provide for appropriate sanctions to be applied if a member is found to have committed a breach. The sanctions may range from a warning or reprimand to suspension and, ultimately, expulsion. It is also sensible to make provision for the member to appeal against the decision.

2.84 Finally, the rules also need to make provision for members to terminate their membership voluntarily, by resigning from the club. This is dealt with in the final part of this section. See para. 2.120.

Non-payment of members' dues

2.85 The rules normally deal with non-payment of dues separately from other breaches and set out a procedure for the Committee to follow when a member does not pay. There are usually two types of dues: payment of an entrance fee and payment of the annual subscription. For the sake of clarity, the rules should deal with new members and continuing members separately.

2.86 It is up to the club to decide whether it wishes to charge an entrance fee. If it does, the rules should set out a timeframe for paying the fee and the steps the club may take in the event of non-payment. So, for example, the rules may say that a member who has not paid the entrance fee within three months will be reported to the Committee who may suspend or terminate membership.

They may also state that the new member will not be allowed to enjoy any of the privileges or facilities of the Club or to vote or act as a member of a committee.

2.87 In the case of payment of the annual subscription, the rules may allow it to be paid quarterly or half-yearly. They should set out a process for dealing with the non-payment by both new members and ongoing members of the annual subscription. So, for example, they may provide:

- for the member to be sent a notice of default and given a period of time to respond, and then
- for the member's name to be posted in the Club;
- for notification of the non-payment and posting to be communicated to the member; and
- for the member to be removed from membership.

2.88 It is important that the rules should set out a procedure for payment (and non-payment) of the member's subscription since the contract of membership does not contain an implied term that membership will lapse in the event of non-payment of the subscription by a specified date. This means that there should be an express rule dealing with non-payment of the subscription.

2.89 A rule dealing with non-payment of the annual subscription might be drafted as follows:

"In the event that the annual subscription or any instalment is not paid within [one] month[s] of the due date, the Secretary shall send the member a written notice of the arrears. If the subscription or any instalment is not paid within [three] months of the due date, the member shall automatically cease to be a member of the Club."

As drafted, the rule provides for automatic lapse of membership. An alternative wording might state that the Secretary could warn the member of the lapse of membership in the event of failure to pay within the stipulated time. That would be a less strict approach.

Breaches of the Rules

2.90 As we have seen, a member of a club has a contractual relationship with all the other members. If he or she breaks one of the club's rules that amounts to a breach of contract. This is because the club's rules contain the terms of the contract. A breach of the rules is, therefore, a breach of contract.

2.91 In view of this, there should be a rule expressly stating that all members are bound by and must comply with the rules and regulations (if any) of the club. Such a rule may state:

> *"No member shall conduct himself or herself within the Clubhouse in a manner which constitutes conduct unbefitting a member of the Club or, whether within or outside the Clubhouse, in a way which brings or is calculated to bring the Club into disrepute."*

Clearly, this sort of rule is likely to give rise to problems of interpretation. Note that the draft above includes the phrases "conduct unbefitting a member of the club", "whether within or outside the Clubhouse" and "brings or is calculated to bring the Club into disrepute". All these phrases are open to interpretation.

2.92 Breaches of the rules may take a variety of different forms and may be minor or serious. They may range from unbecoming conduct on the club's premises to failure to pay the membership subscription. They may also take place on a single occasion or be regular or persistent. The rules therefore need to be flexible and cater for the different outcomes which may follow from breaches of them. This means that there should be an appropriate procedure for investigating any breach and providing for an appropriate sanction.

Disciplinary procedure

2.93 The club's rules need to cater for occasions when a member is alleged to have broken the rules in some way or to have misbehaved in a way which is inappropriate and should have an appropriate procedure for dealing with it. They should make provision for the following matters:

1. what events may trigger the operation of the procedure;
2. who may initiate the procedure;
3. the form of the procedure;
4. sanctions which may be imposed at the conclusion of the procedure; and
5. appeals.

2.94 For each stage of the process there should be specified time limits, to enable the procedure to move forward without unnecessary delay. Sometimes, the rules speak of steps in the procedure being taken within a "reasonable" time frame or of a member being given a "reasonable" opportunity to respond to the procedure. This is to be avoided. Opinions may vary about what is a "reasonable" timeframe. So, therefore, the procedure should specify the number of days for the different steps to be completed.

2.95 Whatever the rules say about applying the procedure, it is important that the committee follows it. Otherwise, in the event of litigation, their decision may be held to be void. Two cases are worth noting here. The first, *Labouchère v Earl of Wharncliffe* (1879), involved a general meeting of committee members of the Beefsteak Club which was called to consider the expulsion of the claimant, Mr Labouchère. A fortnight's notice of such a meeting was required but was not given. The judge held that the committee had no power to expel him as the meeting was irregularly called. (This case is also discussed further below in the context of the giving of correct notices: see para. 3.107.) In similar vein is the case of *Young v Imperial Ladies Club Limited* (1920), which also involved the expulsion of a member. A notice was issued convening a special meeting of the executive committee, but the notice was not sent to one of the members (the Duchess of Abercorn). The reason for this omission was that she had previously indicated that she would not be attending committee meetings because of other calls on her time. The Court of Appeal decided that the omission to summon the absent member invalidated the proceedings. They also said that the notice did not state the object of the meeting adequately.

2.96 Two points follow from this. *First*, the more elaborate the procedure the greater the risk of a failure to observe its requirements and, therefore, of the decision being held by a Court to be null and void. A committee dealing with the discipline of a member needs to take great care to make sure that it observes the rules. In the *Young* case, above, the omission to send the Duchess a notice of the meeting could easily have been cured by sending her a notice despite the fact that she had said that she would not attend meetings. In the *Labouchère* case, the problem was that the notice did not comply with the time limit set out in the rules. So the non-compliance was fatal to the decision to expel the member. *Second*, as a general rule the club should aim to keep its disciplinary procedures as simple as possible. Unless it is a large club or it is a club which has disciplinary functions in relation to the regulation of the particular activity on a national level, it should aim for brevity and simplicity.

Initiating the disciplinary procedure

2.97 First, the rules need to set out the sorts of events which will trigger the operation of the procedure. A rule commonly to be found is one which states that that all members are bound by the rules and regulations of the club and that a member who commits a breach of them may be subject to the procedure. They may also say something like:

> *"No member shall conduct himself or herself within the Clubhouse in a manner which constitutes conduct unbefitting a member of the Club or, whether within or outside the Clubhouse, in a way which brings or is calculated to bring the Club into disrepute."*

Note that this rule applies to a member's conduct *whether or not* it takes place on the club's premises. Note too that the way the rule is phrased – "no member shall conduct himself or herself . . . in a way which brings or is calculated to bring the Club into disrepute" – entails a judgement as to whether the conduct is of such a kind as to bring the club into disrepute. This is looked at in more detail below.

2.98 The rules should also make a distinction between single or minor breaches of the rules and major breaches. Take the example of a member who drinks too much one night and makes a mess in the clubhouse. If the member has no previous record of any such behaviour, the matter should be approached differently from the case of a member who has a record of persistent drunkenness and, when drunk, of rudeness to the club's staff. This means that the rules need to address two separate matters: (1) the case of minor or single breaches of the rules: and (2) the case of major or persistent breaches. In the second case, they need also to consider the question of behaviour outside the club and whether such behaviour brings the member within the rules. For example, in the second case, the rules may state that the procedure may be operated where the member concerned commits "material breaches" of the rules, defined as meaning "any one or more serious or persistent breaches of the rules".

2.99 Once the type of behaviour has been identified, the rules need to address how the procedure may be brought into play. In general, there are three possible means of initiating a procedure:

1. by the committee taking action; or
2. by a group of members making a request for the procedure to be initiated; or
3. as a result of a complaint made to the Secretary by a member of the club's staff about the member's behaviour towards him or her.

So far as this last possibility is concerned, it should be noted that the rules of many clubs do not provide for the possibility of staff complaints against members. If a club's rules do not provide for this, the club should consider introducing regulations to deal with it, particularly if it has quite a large staff. See, further, Ch. 4, para. 4.75.

2.100 After the complaint has been initiated, the rules should then set out a procedure for dealing with it. Whether the member is alleged to have committed trivial breaches or more serious breaches, the procedure needs to be flexible enough to deal with all types of allegations. Whichever of the three methods of initiating a complaint is involved, it is the committee which applies the procedure for dealing with it.

Form of the Procedure

2.101 The procedure should comply with the rules of natural justice, irrespective of the form it takes. These are:

- the right to be heard by an unbiassed tribunal;
- the right to have notice of charges of misconduct; and
- the right to be heard in answer to those charges.

They were stated by Lord Hodson in the seminal case of *Ridge v Baldwin* (1964). Any decision reached by the club which does not comply with these rules will be invalid and liable to be set aside by the court. The rules apply equally to honorary members as well as to ordinary members.

2.102 The *first* step is to give the member notice of the charges and to give him or her the opportunity to make representations in relation to the charges. At this stage, as with the entire procedure, time limits need to be set. So, for example, the member may be required to submit written representations within a specified period of time, for instance 14 days.

2.103 The *next* step is to arrange for the charges to be heard. At this stage, various questions arise. These include the following:

1. Should the matter be dealt with by the entire committee or should a sub-committee be set up to consider the matter?
2. How much notice of the meeting should be given?
3. Should the matter be confined to written representations or should the member be allowed to appear and argue the case in person?
4. If so, should the committee allow witnesses to be heard and cross-examined?
5. Should the member be allowed legal representation or should he or she be allowed only a fellow-member as representative?

2.104 First, a decision should be made as to who will deal with the allegations. Should it be the entire Committee or a sub-committee? In many clubs, the members of the committee or any sub-committee set up to consider the complaint are likely to know the member. This gives rise to the risk of accusations of bias. This is a difficult area, but clearly a committee member who is a friend of the accused should not participate in the meeting which deals with the charge. The test favoured by the courts in such matters is whether "the fair-minded and informed observer, having considered the facts, would conclude that there was a real possibility of bias": see *Porter v Magill* (2002).

2.105 Bearing in mind that the Club may feel it necessary to provide for an appeals process, it is advisable for the allegations to be heard by a sub-committee which then passes its conclusions to the Club's General Committee for the final decision in relation to appropriate sanctions against the member to be taken. Appeals are dealt with at para. 2.116.

2.106 In relation to notice of the meeting, the normal notice would be 14 or 21 days. If the rules did not state the period of notice, notice of a reasonable length would be implied. In practice, that would probably be 14 days.

2.107 A further consideration is the conduct of the meeting. The following questions need to be dealt with:

- Should it be confined to written representations?
- Should the member be allowed to appear and argue the case in person?
- Should legal representation be allowed if the member asks for it?

The rules need to deal with these questions. So far as legal representation is concerned, if the rules do not say anything about legal representation and the member asks for it, the committee has a discretion as to whether to allow it. It would be better, however, if it were expressly dealt with. If legal representation is expressly excluded, that would not be a breach of natural justice.

2.108 Once the committee has concluded the process of conducting a hearing in relation to the complaint against the member, it must then go on to decide on an appropriate sanction.

Sanctions

2.109 The rules should provide for a range of sanction to be available to the committee if it decides that the member charged with misconduct is guilty. Bearing in mind that the misconduct may be minor or serious, the disciplinary procedure needs to cater for these possibilities. It should be stressed that the rules should set out *expressly* the sanctions which may be imposed. They will not be implied.

2.110 The overriding consideration when considering what sanction to impose on the member who has been found guilty of misconduct is whether the proposed sanction is proportional to the misconduct of which he or she has been found guilty. This is the judicial view:

> *"The test of proportionality requires the striking of a balance between competing considerations. The application of the test in the context of penalty will not necessarily produce just one right answer: there is no single "correct" decision. Different decision-makers may come up with different answers, all of them reached in an entirely proper application of the test. . . [T]he decision is unlawful only if it falls outside the range of reasonable responses to the question of where a fair balance lies between the conflicting interests. The same essential approach must apply in a . . . context such as the present. It is for the primary decision-maker to strike the balance in determining whether the penalty is proportionate. The court's role, in the exercise of its supervisory jurisdiction, is to determine whether the decision reached falls within the limits of the decision-maker's discretionary area of judgment. If it does, the penalty is lawful; if it does not, the penalty is unlawful. It is not the role of the court to stand in the shoes of the primary decision-maker, strike the balance for itself and determine on that basis what it considers the right penalty should be."*

See *Bradley v The Jockey Club* (2004). The judge's opinion in that case is set out here in full because it is important that members of a disciplinary committee arrive at a decision which cannot be impeached.

2.111 The following sanctions may be imposed upon a member at the conclusion of a disciplinary procedure:

- fine;
- reprimand, warning or censure;
- suspension; or
- expulsion.

In arriving at its decision, the committee may take into account any previous episodes involving the member. It is sensible to include this expressly in the Rules. An example of suitable wording would be:

*"For the avoidance of doubt in making a determination or decision under [rule **] the Committee may take into account, in so far as it is relevant and appropriate to do so, the fact that the member has previously been censured under this Rule."*

Finally, the Rules should deal with how the Committee's decision should be publicised and whether all decision should be given publicity or merely the decisions to suspend or expel. Again, if the rules do not provide for publicising a warning, for example, it would be a breach of them then to publicise the decision.

2.112 The club's rules should be drafted flexibly, so as to include powers to discipline members for breaches of the rules without going so far as to expel them. In the case of a warning, that may be state that a further breach may lead to the member's expulsion. The power of expulsion should be reserved for serious or persistent breaches of the rules. The third and fourth possible sanctions are looked at here.

2.113 *Suspension* A power to suspend a member should be given expressly in the rules, since a power to expel a member does not include a power to suspend. Suspension of a member means, in effect, that the member loses the privileges and rights of membership during the period of suspension. Since one of the privileges or rights of membership is the holding of office within the club or becoming a member of the committee, that raises the question whether a suspended member may be nominated or elected to an office or to the committee. Similarly, if the member is suspended during the period of office, the question is whether he or she should stand aside during the period of suspension. In both cases, these possibilities should be catered for in the rules.

2.114 The rules should therefore set out the following matters:

- the nature and extent of the member's rights during suspension;
- the length of the suspension; and
- the rights of the suspended member in relation to matters such as standing for election to the committee or continuing as a member of the committee.

2.115 *Expulsion* As with suspension, the rules should make *express* provision for expulsion. The following matters should be deal with:

- the number of members required to be present at the meeting at which the decision to expel is taken; and
- the percentage of members present needed to take the decision.

So, for example, the rules may state that, in the case of a committee with 25 members, at least 20 should be present to enable a decision to expel to be made and, of those 20, at least three quarters should vote in favour of expulsion. Then, as mentioned above (at para.2.111), provision should be made for the decision to be publicised and what form the publicity should take.

Appeals

2.116 In many cases, the decision reached by the Committee will be the end of the matter and it is not necessary for the rules to make provision for an appeal. Inevitably, though, cases occur where it is alleged that there was some sort of defect in the original hearing. That raises the question of how to deal with the problem.

2.117 If the club wishes to have an appeal process – and this may be necessary if the club has a disciplinary function (for example, the Jockey Club or the Kennel Club or the disciplinary panel of a professional association) – then the first step is to create an appropriate appellate panel. The members of the body which took the original decision cannot be members of the body. So, thought needs to be given to the constitution of it. Depending on the structure of the club, the panel might consist of the club's trustees; or of members of the committee who were not present at the original hearing. If the original decision was arrived at by a sub-committee then a separate sub-committee may be set up to deal with the appeal. A further question to consider is whether to allow representation – legal or otherwise. It may be a sensible practice to allow some form of representation.

2.118 The next question is: what is the role of the appellate panel? One possibility is for the panel to send the matter back to the original sub-committee if it is satisfied that there was a defect in the original decision. So, in effect, the original decision is expunged, and the disciplinary process starts afresh. An alternative is for the panel to conduct a complete re-hearing at the appellate level. This is an area where there is a considerable amount of case-law and judicial commentary. One view is that an unfair trial cannot be cured by a fair appeal. On the other hand, Lord Wilberforce has referred to

"... the possibility that, intermediately, the conclusion to be reached, on the rules and on the contractual context, is that those who have joined in an organisation, or contract, should be taken to have agreed to accept what in the end is a fair decision, notwithstanding some initial defect.

... [S]uch intermediate cases exist. In them it is for the Court, in the light of the agreements made, and in addition having regard to the course of proceedings, to decide whether, at the end of the day, there has been a fair result, reached by fair methods, such as the parties *should fairly be taken to have accepted when they joined the association. Naturally there may be instances when the defect is so flagrant, the consequences so severe, that the most perfect of appeals or re-hearings will not be sufficient to produce a just result. . ."*

2.119 Unless the club's rules make specific provision, an appeal is a review of the original decision, not a complete re-hearing. That means that the appellate panel has a restricted role. It is, in effect, to review the integrity of the original hearing.

Termination of membership/resignation

2.120 So far, we have looked at the procedure for dealing with members. Now, it is appropriate to look at the position of a member who wishes to terminate their membership, in other words someone who wishes to resign from the club. This matter is not as simple as it might seem. The following questions arise:

- If there is no express rule dealing with resignation, is it possible for the resignation of a member to be valid?
- What amounts to a resignation?
- Must it be in writing?
- What is the effect of a requested resignation?

2.121 First, in the absence of express provision in the rules, a member has the right to resign from the club and cannot be restrained from doing so. The rules may provide for the method of resignation, for example by a requirement that is in writing or that it should be with 14 days' notice or at a specified time of the year, for example before 31 December. A suitable rule might say something like:

"The Committee may accept the resignation of any member to take effect from 1st January following subject to written notice having been received by the Secretary of the Club before that date."

This could be amended in order to include a requirement for the resignation to be in writing.

2.122 It is not always clear from a club's rules how a member may go about resigning. Sometimes, the procedure for resignation is to be found in the section relating to payment of subscriptions. Ideally, it should be in that part of the rules which deals with other matters relating to membership, such as admission/election, non-payment of dues and the like.

2.123 No particular form of words is required to amount to a valid resignation. The judicial view of this is as follows:

> ". . . There can be no magic in the word 'resign', nor in whether the resignation is written or oral. The essence of the matter seems to me to be whether the member has sufficiently manifested his decision to be a member no more. . . [T]he only question is whether the member's decision has been adequately conveyed . . . by words or deeds."

See *In re Sick and Funeral Society of St John's Sunday School, Golcar* (1973).

2.124 The final point to look at here is the question of forced resignations or invitations to resign. A genuine invitation to resign is a useful option available to a committee where a member's behaviour has been unacceptable. It is a useful and face-saving option for a club which wishes to deal with an awkward situation. On the hand, a forced resignation would amount to an expulsion without the appropriate procedure having been gone through. That would expose the club to the argument that the expulsion was invalid as being in breach of the rules.

Resolution of disputes

2.125 Inevitably disagreements arise in a club and some end up before the courts. Some of the cases mentioned in Chapter 1 involved disagreements between members and the club, and, in the absence of internal resolution of the disagreements, litigation followed. Examples are *Thellusson v Viscount Valentia* (involving the Hurlingham Club), *Baker v Jones* (involving the British Amateur Weightlifters' Association) and *Harington v Sendall* (involving the Oxford and Cambridge Club).

2.126 Litigation will inevitably lead to unwelcome publicity, particularly if the club is well known. It is preferable, therefore, for the club to try to resolve any dispute privately. This will involve having a rule which provides for private dispute resolution – either mediation or arbitration.

2.127 It is not possible for the rules to prevent a member resorting to litigation in the event of a dispute. Such a rule would be void. It is possible, though, to have a rule which provides for private dispute resolution. A rule of this sort might say:

"Any dispute involving the Club and/or the members shall be referred to the arbitration of a sole arbitrator to be appointed in accordance with section 16(3) of the Arbitration Act 1996. If the parties fail to make such an appointment, the appointment shall be made by the President of the Chartered Institute of Arbitrators. The arbitrator shall decide the dispute according to the laws of England and Wales. This rule does not prevent the dispute being referred to mediation for resolution prior to arbitration."

2.128 The effect of such a rule is that a dispute would have to be resolved by arbitration or mediation machinery without recourse to the courts. If a member tried to ignore or bypass the rule, the club could apply to the court to ask it to delay the proceedings under section 6 of the Arbitration Act 1996. Section 6(4) obliges the Court to do this unless it is satisfied that "the arbitration agreement is null and void, inoperative, or incapable of being performed". A rule of the sort set out above would not be caught by that provision.

2.129 If the rules do not contain a rule dealing with dispute resolution, it will not be possible to imply a term dealing with the resolution of the dispute. But that would not prevent the parties to the dispute agreeing to some form of private dispute resolution.

3. The Management and Running of the Club

Introduction

3.1 This chapter deals with the management and running of the Club. First of all, it looks at the people involved in the running of the club; then it discusses meetings, which are the means by which the members control the running of the club.

3.2 The people who may be involved fall into three groups:

- Trustees;
- Officers; and
- Committee.

Much depends on the size of the club. Trustees will need to be appointed only if the club owns or leases property. The number of people in the second group – the Officers – will also depend on the size of the club. A large club may decide to have a President and Vice-Presidents, whereas a small club may not feel the need for them.

3.3 The third group – the Committee – is the most important in practice. Although in theory all the members of the club have an equal say in the management of the club, in reality it would be impossible to run a club of any size without delegating the members' powers of management to officers and to a committee. Since the day-to-day management of the club is in the hands of the committee, most of the chapter will deal with that group of people.

3.4 The final section of the chapter discusses meetings. This topic is important since it is the members who control the club; they elect those of their number who will be responsible for running the club. Ultimately, they are responsible for the direction and development of the club.

Trustees

3.5 The club will only need to appoint trustees if it owns property, whether the property is freehold or held on a lease ("leasehold"). Since a club, as we have seen, has no legal personality (unlike a company), it cannot hold property in its own name. Some clubs do not need premises to conduct their activities. Others do. Clearly, a sports club will not be able to function without premises on which to conduct its activities. On the other hand, a club such as a reading group or sewing circle does not need dedicated premises to operate. The term "property" covers the premises and land on which the club operates. But it also includes what is called "personal property". This is property other than land, such as paintings, furniture and the like.

3.6   If the club does own property – whether it owns the property outright or leases it – it needs to have trustees to hold that property. So named individuals must be appointed to hold it (whether it is freehold or leasehold) on behalf of the members. These people are named as trustees and the members of the club are the beneficiaries. It would be unworkable for the entire membership to be named as owners of the land or grantees of the lease. For that reason, the law makes provision for a small number of persons to be registered as trustees: they will be the registered owners of the freehold or registered grantees of the lease. They are called trustees, since they hold the property *on trust* for the members of the club. Their obligations are governed by the law of Trusts.

3.7   The nature of the trust in this context is what is called a "bare" trust. This type of trust arises where the trustee holds the property for an adult beneficiary absolutely. In the case of a club, the trustees hold the property on trust for the members of the club (who are the beneficiaries under the trust). They hold the property in accordance with the rules of the club and under the direction of the committee. Their control over the property is limited and they are not obliged to carry out any active duties as trustees. They are subject to the direction of the beneficiaries (the members of the club), acting through the committee. The existence of the trustees is to do with the need for title to the property to be held by a small number of named persons. It has no bearing on the contractual relationship between the members of the club. Effectively, the trustees may remain in the background and need have no involvement in the management of the club.

3.8 Even so, the club's rules should make provision for the trustees. They should deal with the following matters:

- the appointment, retirement and removal of the trustees;
- the relationship of the trustees with the club; and
- attendance at committee meetings.

In relation to the third point, if the trustees are entitled to attend committee meetings, then consideration must be given to whether they may actively participate in the conduct of the meetings and whether they may take part in a vote. There is no obligation on the club to include them in the running of the club. The point is that the rules need to be clear about their role. If the rules do not specify a role for the trustees, then they would not be entitled to attend committee meetings or be involved in the management of the club.

3.9 A further point to note is that, if the trustees were to be involved in the business of the club's committee, they would be exposed to the risk of liability in the same way as members of the committee: see para. 3.95, below. For this reason, it is best that they should remain in the background.

Officers

Introduction

3.10 The officers of the club are usually the Chairman/Chair, the Secretary and the Treasurer. Some clubs may also choose to have positions such as Patron, President, Vice-President and the like. Those selected are likely to have been chosen for ornamental reasons and, in practice, are unlikely to be involved in the management and running of the club. It is also likely that only larger organisations will choose to have such officers.

3.11 If the rules of the club provide for such officers, the rules should be clear as to their role. They should also deal with matters such as:

- method of selection;
- duration of term of office; and
- role (if any) in the management and running of the club.

Election and tenure of officers

3.12 Practices vary in relation to the election and tenure of officers. So far as a President and Vice-Presidents are concerned – if the club has such officers – then it is sensible to grant these titles for a limited duration. Otherwise, it may be difficult to remove a President or Vice-President elected for an unspecified term. A time limit should be attached to the term of office.

3.13 So far as the other officers are concerned, practices vary. The following methods of selection are possible:

- election of the officers by the members in general meeting;
- appointment by the committee; or
- election by the members but on the recommendation of the committee.

In the first case, the rules should provide for a process of nomination, for example that the nominee is proposed and seconded by members of the club. In the last case, if the members rejected the committee's recommendation, they would not be able to elect their own candidate. They would need to await a fresh recommendation from the committee.

3.14 So far as the election of the Chairman is concerned, it is common in many clubs for the committee to elect as Chairman one of their number immediately after the general meeting. In other clubs, the nomination for Chairman is open to the whole membership and the election takes place at the Annual General Meeting. Similar considerations apply in the case of the Secretary and Treasurer.

3.15 The difference between the two methods is this:

- a person elected by the committee after the AGM holds that office until the meeting of the new committee after the next AGM; but
- a person elected at the AGM holds office until the next AGM.

3.16 Whatever the method of election, it is important that the rules are clear.

Chairman/chair

3.17 The first point to make is that the word 'Chairman' has a male connotation; this can be a sensitive issue. In practice, it is best left to the person concerned to decide how he or she would prefer to be addressed. In this book, the person is referred to as the Chairman.

3.18 There is a distinction between the chairman of the club and the chairman of the committee. They are usually the same, but, for the sake of clarity, the rules should state that fact. The chairman of the committee is, as the title implies, the person who chairs meetings of the committee.

3.19 On the other hand, the Chairman of the *club* is responsible, together with the Secretary and the Treasurer, for ensuring the smooth running of the club. In view of the fact that meetings of the committee are likely to take place only once a month, on a day-to-day basis these three officers are likely to be responsible for the running of the club. This is a common way of proceeding. The rules should make clear, though, that any important decisions should be reported to the next meeting of the committee and ratified by the committee.

3.20 One matter should be noted here. Bearing in mind that the Chairman is likely to be involved in the day-to-day running of the club, thought should be given to whether the rules should give him/her authority to act on behalf of the club. For example, the rules might expressly allow the Chairman – possible acting with the Secretary or one or two other members of the committee – to enter into contracts. If so, the rules should set a limit to the amount of money he/she may be allowed to commit with referring back to the committee.

Secretary

3.21 In many clubs the title of the secretary is 'Honorary Secretary'. This is because the role is unpaid. In larger clubs, the position is paid and the secretary will be, in effect, the chief executive of the club. In that case, he or she will be an employee of the club and will have a contract of employment which will set out the duties of the post. A paid secretary will report to the committee, but, in practice, the day-to-day running of the club will be in his or her hands. In clubs which have a paid secretary, such as golf clubs, the secretary will be the visible figure of authority. He or she should not be a member of the club.

3.22 An unpaid Secretary, on the other hand, *will* be a member of the club. He or she will be responsible for the due administration of the club: for making sure that membership lists are kept up-to-date, that subscriptions are collected, and that arrangements for the AGM are properly handled, for liaising with the club's committee and for preparing a report of the club's activities since the previous AGM. It is sensible for the rules to provide that the Secretary should be a member of the club.

3.23 As in the case of the Chairman, it is sensible for the rules to deal with the issue of the extent of his/her authority to act on behalf of the club.

Treasurer

3.24 The Treasurer is responsible for the financial affairs of the club. In a small club, the office will be honorary in the sense that the person holding it is unpaid. A larger club, on the other hand, may have a paid accounts manager or finance director who reports to a finance committee or the club's managing committee and is an employee of the club.

3.25 The Treasurer is responsible for preparing the club's accounts for members at the AGM and is also responsible for making sure that financial matters are properly handled and the club's funds are spent solely on club purposes.

3.26 As with the Secretary, if the office of Treasurer is honorary, the rules should provide that he or she should be a member of the club.

Committee

Introduction

3.27 The Committee is the group of members elected by their fellow-members to manage the affairs of the club. The election usually takes place at the Annual General Meeting, but may take place on a separate occasion. This group may have different names: "Management Committee", "Executive Committee", "General Committee", "Committee". Other names are also to be found, for example "Council", "General Council". Irrespective of the title used in the Constitution/Rules of the Club, this group is responsible for the management and running of the club. It is simplest here to call them the "Committee".

3.28 The committee is elected by the members and the powers of control and management of the club are delegated to them by the members. This means that the actions taken by the members of the committee are taken on behalf of the membership as a whole. When the committee or some of its members take an action on behalf of the club – for example, entering into a contract with a third party – they are acting on behalf of the club. Since, however, the club is not a legal person (see para. 1.2), the person(s) entering into the contract on its behalf will be taken to have contracted in a personal capacity. They cannot be the agents of the club, since it is not possible for an agent to act on behalf of a principal which does not have legal capacity.

3.29 In these kinds of dealings, the law of agency is involved. Therefore, if the committee decides to enter into a contract with a third party and authorises one or more of its members to deal with the third party, that group will be acting as agents of the committee in their dealings with the third party. Under the law of agency, the act of the agent is the act of the principal. In other words, the committee – who in this example are the principals – are liable for the acts of the group (their agents) who contract with the third party. This means that the committee will be a party to the contract and liable under it to the person with whom it was made. The committee cannot be said to be the agents of the club, since it has no legal personality. This is a difficult issue which is examined more fully later in the chapter: see para. 3.73 below.

3.30 The club's rules need to deal expressly with the functioning of the committee. This is important since the committee may only exercise the power given to it by the rules and its members need to be clear as to what they can and cannot do. In addition to the express rules, though, there will also arise implied duties. These, as we saw in Chapter 1 (see para. 1.25), come into play to deal with situations which fall outside the express rules. But they can only come into play if there is no express rule dealing with the matter; if there is an express rule, there is no place for them. An example is the committee's general duty of care to the members: see para. 3.52, below.

3.31 This section looks at the following matters:

- the composition and operation of the committee;
- method of selection of the committee;
- meetings of the committee;
- duties of the committee;
- powers of the committee; and
- liability of the committee members.

Composition and operation of the committee

3.32 In selecting a committee to run their affairs, the members of the club are delegating their powers of control to the whole committee. That means that the rules must state how the powers of the committee may be exercised. For example, if they did not give a power to reach a decision by means of a quorum, any decisions would need to be arrived at by the entire committee. That would make the operation of the committee difficult. Similarly, in relation to co-option. If the rules made no provision for the committee to change its composition, the committee would have no power of co-option. On the other hand, the committee has the power to decide on its own procedures and how it will operate.

3.33 So, the rules should state how many members are to be on the committee and how they should be chosen. They need to deal with the following matters:

- eligibility to be a committee member;
- method of selection of committee members;
- number of members;
- length of term of membership;
- maximum number of terms;
- lapse of membership;
- meetings of the committee;
- powers of the committee; and
- conflicts of interest.

It is important to remember that if the rules do not deal with a matter, then the committee has no power in relation to it. That is why it is important to make sure that the rules cover matters such as quoracy and co-option. The only way to give the committee a power it does not have is to amend the rules, but this cannot be done retrospectively and can only be dealt with it at the Annual General Meeting or an Extraordinary General Meeting.

3.34 An example of a possible rule dealing with the composition of the committee is:

(a) *"The affairs of the Club shall be managed by a Committee of **fifteen ordinary** members, of whom **five shall form a quorum**. The Committee shall have **power to co-opt** not more than three members of the Club as advisers who shall be in addition to the fifteen members referred to above but **such co-opted members shall have no voting power and shall be co-opted for no longer than until 1st January the following year. The Trustees of the Club shall have the right to attend all meetings of the Committee but shall not be entitled to vote**.*

(b) *"Each member of the Committee shall be elected in accordance with the provisions of Rule * to serve on the Committee for a term of three years from 1st January following election. No member of the*

Committee who has served for two consecutive terms then about to be completed may be nominated for re-election."

Note the following points relating to the highlighted text:

1. the number of members is set at 15;
2. the members eligible for election are *ordinary* members, not, for example, honorary members;
3. the quorum is set at five, i.e. one third of the entire committee;
4. the committee has a power of co-option;
5. the co-opted members have no voting powers and may only be co-opted for a limited time;
6. the term of a member is set at three years with a maximum of two terms, i.e. six years' maximum; and
7. the trustees have the right to attend committee meetings but are not entitled to vote.

Note that the rule set out above is only an example of the sort of rule a club might have. There is no right answer to how many members a club's committee should have or what the quorum should be. What is important is to ensure that the committee is not so large that it becomes unwieldy.

Sub-committees

3.35 The Committee has the power to appoint sub-committees, though in practice it is sensible for the rules to set out the committee's powers in relation to sub-committees. This is dealt with at para. 3.63, below.

Lapse of membership

3.36 It is important that the members of the committee take an active role in running the affairs of the club. For this reason, it is sensible to make provision in the rules for membership of the committee to lapse if the committee member does not attend a specified number of meetings. So, for example, the rules may say:

"Any member of the Committee who has ceased to be a member of the Club or who has failed to attend three consecutive meetings of the

Committee in any year shall cease to be a member of the Committee, provided that in the latter case the Committee shall have power to re-instate such member if, in its opinion, non-attendance has been justified."

If there were no such rule, it would not be possible to remove a member for non-attendance.

Method of selection of the committee

3.37 The example rule set out above states that each member of the committee is to be elected in accordance with the provisions of a separate rule. Although committee members might be selected by other means (for example, nomination), it is normal for them to go through a process of election. The election usually takes place at the Annual General Meeting, but there is no reason why the rules should not provide for the election to take place at a different time.

3.38 The rules may provide for members of the club to put themselves up as candidates, subject to nomination requirements – for example, a proposer and seconder. An alternative would be for the rules to provide for members of the existing committee to recommend candidates for election. In this case, if the members rejected the recommended candidates, they would not have power to proceed to their own election but would have to await further recommendations from the committee. As an alternative to a member putting his or her name forward, it would be feasible for the committee to put forward their own candidates for election. In any event, the process of nomination should be dealt with in the rules.

3.39 The rule relating to the election of the committee should set out how the election is to be conducted. The following questions need to be considered:

- How much notice of the election should be given?
- What are the requirements for nomination of a candidate (for example, proposer/seconder/supporters)?
- What details of the candidates should be made available?

- How should the details be publicised?
- How should the election be conducted? By post only or by electronic means or by a combination of the two?
- Should scrutineers be appointed to oversee the operation of the election?

3.40 So far as *notice* of the meeting is concerned, it is important to make sure that the rules relating to the requisite length of notice are complied with. See para. 3.107, below, for a discussion of the case of *Labouchère v Earl of Wharncliffe*. That case makes clear that if the notice requirements are not complied with the meeting will be invalid.

3.41 In relation to the results of the election, the rules need to cater for matters such as:

- publication of the results;
- the total number of votes cast; and
- the number of votes cast for each candidate.

It is not necessary to publicise the number of votes cast for each candidate and the club may prefer that this aspect of the election should remain undisclosed.

Meetings of the committee

3.42 The committee members act on behalf of the membership as a whole in the decisions they take relating to the running of the club, particularly those decisions which involve dealings with third parties, for example outside contractors engaged to do work on the club's premises. This means that the rules should make provision for the conduct of committee meetings. For example, the committee might make a controversial decision with which several of its members disagreed. This might give rise to questions as to whether the meeting was properly constituted, whether a quorum was present and whether the decision reached had the required majority. It is important that the rules deal with these matters as clearly as possible. If they do so, then the scope for future dissent will be reduced.

3.43 The committee may decide on its own procedures. So, for example, it may appoint a sub-committee or working party; it may also delegate a task to an individual or group of individual committee members. When it does this, it is important that it requires those to whom it has made a delegation to report their activities to the committee for approval and ratification. The reason for this is that the whole committee is responsible for the club's affairs and is answerable to the membership. It is to the *entire* committee that the members of the club have delegated their powers of control.

3.44 The rules of the club should therefore deal clearly with meetings of the committee. The matters that they should cover are:

- regularity of meetings;
- quorum required;
- majority required for decisions;
- attendance of members;
- authority of members;
- delegation; and
- records of meetings.

3.45 It would be normal for the rules to state that committee meetings should be held monthly and that a record should be kept of the meetings in the form of minutes. In relation to the minutes, consideration should be given as to whether the minutes should be made available to the members of the club. In the interests of transparency, it would be sensible to make provision for them to be reasonably accessible. The possible effect of the Data Protection legislation should be noted. See para. 2.47 above.

3.46 The question of a *quorum* needs to be dealt with. For a committee with a membership of fifteen, the rules may stipulate a quorum of five. They might also go on to say that all decisions of the committee may be reached by a simple majority of those present at the meeting. It would make the working of the committee difficult if the majority required was a majority of the entire committee.

Attendance of members

3.47 Until recently, it was the norm that members of the committee would attend meetings in person. In the absence of a rule allowing for attendance other than in person, it is likely that attendance via any other means would not count as attendance. Since practices have now changed and meetings are often conducted via Zoom or Microsoft Teams or similar electronic methods, the rules should expressly deal with how members may attend committee meetings, if only to avoid arguments that a meeting conducted electronically was not properly conducted.

3.48 It is also important to make provision for handling matters which need to be dealt with urgently. If an emergency arises between the dates fixed for committee meetings, there should be a procedure for dealing with it. The following questions need to be considered:

- Should authority be given to named members (for example, the Chairman and two members of the committee) to act?
- If so, how? By email? By Zoom/Teams?
- Should provision be made for aspects of the committee's business to be conducted by email?
- If so, which aspects?

It is important that these issues should be dealt with expressly in the rules, since, in the absence of express provision, a decision reached in this way would be open to challenge as being invalid.

Authority of committee members

3.49 As we shall see, it is likely that some or all of the committee members will enter into contracts with third parties such as outside contractors. When they do so, they will be liable to the third party since they will be acting as "principals". This terminology is used because the law of agency is involved. To avoid arguments about whether those who took a particular decision had authority to do so, it is sensible that the rules should deal with this question. For example, the rules might authorise the committee to give authority to a specified number of committee members – or to the Chairman – to enter into contracts up to a specified monetary limit. They might also specify the types of contracts that might be entered into. The Rules should make clear that those given authority should be required to report back to the Committee and, if necessary, to ask for ratification of their actions. This is discussed further at para. 3.73 below.

Delegation

3.50 It is likely that the rules would give power to the committee to appoint sub-committees, which are also likely to have authority to deal with third parties. For example, the club's Wine Sub-committee would have authority to buy wine for the club. So too, the rules might empower the committee to delegate certain responsibilities to one or more of its members. When the committee decides to delegate certain tasks, it is important that it requires those to whom it has made a delegation to report their activities to the committee for approval and ratification. Sub-committees are dealt with at para. 3.63 below.

Duties of the committee

3.51 Bearing in mind that the club's rules are unlikely to spell out the relationship between the members of the committee and the other members of the club, the question to be examined is what duties they have towards their fellow-members. In the absence of express provision in the rules, the question is what duties are to be implied. This section should be read together with the two following sections, particularly paras. 3.73 to 3.92 (Powers relating to dealings with third parties) and paras. 3.95 to 3.101 (Liability of Committee Members).

3.52 The members of the committee are regarded as having a duty of care towards their fellow members. This is because, in managing the club's affairs, their relationship with their fellow-members is not merely a social relationship. Amongst other things, they are responsible – with the other members of the committee – for overseeing the financial management of the club. In *Hedley Byrne & Co Ltd v Heller* (1964), one of the judges (Lord Reid) commented that a duty of care arises when there is a business connection between the parties, as opposed to a social one. He said:

> ". . . [I]f someone possessed of a special skill undertakes, quite irrespective of contract, to apply that skill for the assistance of another person who relies upon such skill, a duty of care will arise. . . Furthermore, if in a sphere in which a person is so placed that others could reasonably rely on his judgement or his skill or upon his ability to make careful inquiry, a person is so placed that others could reasonably rely upon his judgment or his skill or upon his ability to make careful inquiry, a person takes it upon himself to give information or advice to, or allows his information or advice to be passed on to, another person who, as he knows or should know, will place reliance upon it, then a duty of care will arise."

3.53 It is clear, therefore, that the members of the committee owe a duty of care to their fellow-members of the club. This gives rise to two questions:

1. What does the duty of care consist of?
2. What is the standard of care required of the committee members?

3.54 A failure to take action might amount to a breach of the *duty of care*. For example, the club has leasehold premises upon which the lease is due to expire. The members in general meeting authorise the committee to negotiate a renewal with the landlord but, because of other distractions and delays, the new lease costs the club a higher premium than would have been the case had the committee acted more promptly. This omission to act more promptly would expose the committee to an action by the members of the club.

3.55 In taking decisions relating to the management of the club the committee must act for the benefit of the club as a whole and not some faction within the membership. The *standard of care* required of the committee is that which might reasonably be expected in all the circumstances. This means that it is necessary to take into account the nature of the club and the sorts of tasks the committee is expected to undertake. There is a vast difference between a national organisation such as the Football Association and a social club in the local village. Clearly, too, a committee may reasonably be expected to give more thought and care to a costly building project than to the organisation of the club's annual dinner. In taking these decisions, members of the committee are acting as "gratuitous agents": they are serving as committee members without being paid.

3.56 The committee members' duty of care means that a committee member should attend committee meetings regularly and should participate actively in the running of the club's affairs. This is the basis for the rule that a committee member who is absent from three consecutive meetings without an accepted apology will cease to be a member of the committee: see para. 3.36, above, for an example of such a rule.

3.57 A further question arises in relation to the liability of the committee. If the decision in question was taken unanimously by the committee then liability will fall on the entire committee. On the other hand, if one or more of the members disagreed with the decision but were outvoted, then it is likely that liability would not fall on those members. Further questions arise here. If a committee member takes no active part in the discussions leading up to the decision because of illness or absence on business, then he or she would probably be in the same position as the members who were outvoted. On the other hand, if he or she attended the meeting but took no active part and abstained in the vote, this would arguably be acquiescence in the decision of the majority.

3.58 This is a difficult area, mainly because there is little authority to give guidance. The old case of *Todd v Emly* (1841) is commonly referred to for guidance in these sorts of situations. In that case, the judge suggested that, if members of a committee are acting together for a "common purpose", then each member of the committee has authority to bind the other members involved in the common purpose. If that is correct, that would mean that in most cases dissentient, absent or abstaining members could still be held liable.

Powers of the committee

3.59 In this section two groups of powers need to be discussed. The first group relates to the operation of the club; the second relates to the wider question of dealings between the committee and third parties.

Powers relating to the management of the club

3.60 Some of these have been touched on earlier: see para. 3.42 above. Possible powers include:

- to elect the chairman;
- to co-opt members to the committee;
- to appoint sub-committees;
- to make regulations; and
- to fill vacancies on the committee.

This group of powers relates to the operation of the committee and the internal regulation of the club.

Election of chairman

3.61 The Chairman may either be elected by the members in general meeting or by the members of the committee. In either case, the rules need to deal with the matter, as well as matters such as the duration of the chairman's tenure.

Co-option to the committee

3.62 Those drafting the rules should give thought to whether they wish to give the committee the power of co-option. The committee may wish to co-opt members with particular expertise to advise on particular issues. If so, the following matters should be dealt with:

- The number of possible co-opted members
- The duration of their membership of the committee, for example for one year only
- Whether they have the power to vote
- Whether they should be a member of the club.

Appointment of sub-committees

3.63 Similar considerations arise in relation to sub-committees. So, questions which need to be dealt with are:

- Should membership of the sub-committee in question be confined to members of the club?
- Should the Chairman of the club be entitled to attend meetings of the sub-committees?
- Should chairmen of sub-committees be entitled to attend the meetings of other sub-committees?
- Who should choose the chairmen of the sub-committees?
- Should the sub-committees have the power of co-option?
- If so, should they exercise the power with the agreement of the Committee?
- If so, should the co-opted members of the sub-committee be members of the club?
- Should the co-opted members have voting powers?
- How long should the co-opted members remain members of the sub-committee?

These questions should be dealt with in the rules since, particularly in the case of a large club, there is a risk of the various sub-committees failing to observe a uniform procedure.

3.64 An example of a rule empowering the committee to appoint sub-committees is:

"The Committee may at any time appoint from its own body as many sub-committees as it deems fit to superintend the several departments of the Club and its activities. With the consent of the General Committee any sub-committee so appointed shall have power to co-opt members of the Club as advisers, but such co-opted members shall have no voting powers."

3.65 The rules should state that all sub-committees should conduct their business in accordance with directions from the committee and that they should regularly report their proceedings to the committee for approval and ratification.

Making regulations or byelaws

3.66 This is an important power, since it enables the committee to regulate the day-to-day running of the club without having to fall back on the rules. In some clubs the regulations are called "byelaws" and in others they are called "regulations". Whichever terminology is used, they amount to the same thing. They are rules made by the committee by virtue of a power given to it in the club's rules. In some cases, the club's rules require the committee to submit a draft of the regulations to a meeting of members for approval. In others, the power is given to the committee without the need for ratification in a general meeting.

3.67 The use of regulations enables the committee to change the regulations from time to time without having to go through the process of changing the rules. As we have seen, changes to the rules need to be dealt with at an Annual General Meeting or Extraordinary General Meeting, which is a slower and more cumbersome process. Such meetings involve formalities, such as notice requirements, which need to be observed. On the other hand, if the committee has a power to make and amend regulations, this is a much less cumbersome and more flexible process.

3.68 What, therefore, should be in the rules and what should be in the regulations? There is no clear answer to this question and different clubs may adopt different approaches. For example, one club's rules may stipulate that the annual subscription should be agreed by the members at an annual Extraordinary General Meeting, whereas another's rules may give power to the committee to set the annual subscription by regulation. The point to bear in mind is that changing the regulations is easier than changing the rules. On the other hand, though, it is important that the fundamental rules of the club may only be amended by the club's members in general meeting. On the whole, it is better for the club to use regulations for its day-to-day running, for example dress codes, opening times, restrictions on the number of guests introduced by the member and the like. See para. 1.11 where this matter is also discussed. At the end of the day, what is important is that the rules make clear which matters must be decided by all the members and which matters may be delegated. If the committee is given power to make a decision, that decision binds the members.

3.69 A rule giving the power to the committee to make regulations might be worded as follows:

> *"The Committee may also from time to time make (and alter) such other Regulations (consistent with these Rules) as it shall think necessary for the well-being of the Club."*

In exercising its power under a rule such as the one above, the overriding considerations for the committee would have to be:

1. whether the proposed regulation was *consistent* with the club rules; and
2. whether the proposed regulation was *for the well-being* of the club.

Any member or group of members who objected to the proposed regulation would have to be able to argue that the proposed change failed on either or both of the two grounds set out above. In that case, the proposed regulation would be said to be *ultra vires* the rules; in other words, that it was outside the power given by the rules.

3.70 Examples of possible regulations are regulations:

- relating to payment of the entrance fee (if any) and the annual subscription;
- relating to opening hours of the clubhouse and the club's facilities, e.g. bar and restaurant (if any);
- relating to dress codes, use of mobile phones and laptop computers;
- dealing with the treatment by members of the club's staff; and
- relating to guests.

3.71 A club which employs staff in any numbers should consider introducing regulations (if it does not already have them) relating to treatment of the staff by members of the club. If it does, it should set out a procedure for dealing with staff complaints. In the event of a staff member making a complaint, the fact the club has regulations of this sort will be useful in the event of any litigation relating to their dismissal or to allegations of unlawful discrimination. See, further, Ch.4, paras. 4.69 to 4.75 and 4.82 to 4.86.

Filling vacancies

3.72 As with the other powers discussed above, it is sensible to have a rule relating to casual vacancies, whether on the Committee itself or on sub-committees. Such a rule might say, for example:

> *"Whenever a casual vacancy shall occur in the membership of any committee, such committee may co-opt another member to fill the vacancy during the period for which the member whose place is to be filled has been elected. Any such co-opted member shall enjoy full voting powers as if directly elected to the committee."*

Note the following points:

1. the duration of the co-opted member's membership lasts only so long as the tenure of the original member's membership of the committee; and
2. the co-opted member has the same voting powers as the member being replaced.

Powers relating to dealings with third parties

3.73 The powers discussed in this section relate to the dealings of the committee with third parties. Examples of the exercise of this power are the employment of staff and entering into contracts with service providers. When the committee decides to enter into a contract, its members are personally liable, on behalf of the club, because they are held to be the principals. This means that the committee members – not the members of the club – are personally liable to the full extent of the contract. As was discussed above (at para. 3.28), the committee members cannot be acting as agents of the club since the club has no legal personality. They must therefore be acting as principals.

3.74 In practice, it is unlikely that the entire committee will be involved. Instead, they will authorise one or more of their number – or, perhaps, the club Secretary – to act on their behalf. In that case, the committee are said to be the principals and the person(s) authorised the agents. The questions which follow from this are examined in this section.

Decision to approve

3.75 The committee is charged with managing the affairs of the club. Its members are obliged to act collectively and they must approve actions taken or to be taken by one of their number. This may be by means of a vote at a regular meeting or at a meeting convened specially for the purpose. So, for example, if the committee decides to engage contractors to do work on the club's premises, they may authorise one or more of their number to sign the contract. They may also vote to give powers to the Chairman to act on their behalf. This might be either for a single purpose – of signing a particular contract – or the more general purpose of signing contracts with service providers.

3.76 A decision to approve an action by one or more members on behalf of the committee may be made by a simple majority. So, if the rules specify that a quorum at a committee meeting is five, that means that a decision may be made by a simple majority of those attending the meeting. It does not require a majority of the entire committee.

Conflicts of interest

3.77 One matter of crucial importance relates to conflicts of interest. These are likely to arise, for example, when the committee decides that certain work needs to be done and a member of the committee who is engaged in that type of work offers to carry out the work. There is likely to be a conflict between the club's interest in having the work well done at as low a cost as possible and the contractor's business interests to maximise the profit from a job. The best way to deal with this kind of situation is for the committee to make sure that all possible conflicts are properly disclosed and recorded in the minutes and that any decision relating to the work is take in the absence of the member.

Agency

3.78 When it comes to organising and entering into contracts, the committee will usually rely upon one or more of its members to carry this out. So the committee may authorise the club secretary or Chairman to do this. In that case, the person(s) appointed will be acting as the agent(s) of the committee. The law of agency will therefore be involved. What this means, as we have seen, is that the contract entered into by the agent is the contract of the principal. In our example, the committee is the principal and the club secretary the agent. The agent has power to bind the principal. Once the contract has been entered into the agent drops out of the picture and the principal is bound.

3.79 What needs to be established in this sort of case is that the agent had the power to take the action. In other words, did the agent have the authority to act on the principal's behalf? Agency may be established by showing that the agent had one of the following types of authority:

1. actual authority;
2. apparent authority; or
3. usual authority.

If it turns out that the agent did not have authority to act, then the next question to consider is whether the agent's actions were ratified by the principal (in this case, the committee): see para. 3.86 below.

3.80 *Actual authority* is usually express but may be implied. It is established where the principal gives the agent the ability to act on its behalf either generally or in relation to specific matters. This may be by means of spoken words or in writing. Clearly, though, it is best practice for the authority to be given in writing. If the agent did not have express authority, then it is necessary to consider whether they had apparent authority. Implied authority arises where the germs of the express authority are incomplete or where the agent has a discretion as to how to act. For example, the agent is authorised to take out insurance but is left to select a suitable policy. Here, the agent has implied authority to select a particular policy.

3.81 *Apparent authority* is sometimes also known as 'ostensible authority'. It arises where the circumstances make it appear to others that a person has authority to act as agent. Thus, the Chairman of a Club will have apparent authority to act (as will the Managing Director of a company). An example is the situation where the Committee of a club elects a new Chairman and gives that person authority to enter into contracts to a maximum value of £5,000. The Chairman enters into a contract worth £20,000. Clearly, he has actual authority to enter the contract. But the question is whether he or she had apparent authority to enter into the particular contract worth £20,000. He/she will have apparent authority if it can be shown that £20,000 is within the usual authority of the Chairman of a club. If, in fact, the action was outside the scope of the Chairman's apparent authority, the next question is whether the action was ratified by the committee (who in this case would be the principal).

3.82 *Usual authority* means the authority which agents of the type concerned usually have in a particular trade or business. It arises where the agent is appointed to some position or office. There is an overlap between implied and apparent authority. The third party cannot sue the principal if he/she knew of the limitations of the agency.

3.83 Of the three types of authority set out above, clearly it is preferable to be able to show that the agent had express authority. Even so, though, there are further questions to be dealt with. The two main questions are:

1. whether the agent had authority in relation to the particular type of contract; and
2. whether the authority had a financial limit.

So, for example, the agent (for example, the club Secretary) enters into a contract to re-furbish the club's kitchens. The cost turns out to be £250,000. So, the questions here are:

1. did he or she have authority to enter that particular contract; and
2. was he/she authorised to enter into a contract for that amount?

3.84 The exercise of authority by agents is subject to three main restraints:

1. they may only act within the scope of their authority;
2. they must exercise the power for the purpose for which it was given; and
3. they must act in what they consider to be the best interests of the club.

So that they may assess and do what is in the best interests of the club, they must fully inform themselves of all the material information relevant to the decision.

3.85 The consequence is that if one or more members of the committee act outside the scope of their authority, the other members may not be bound by the action of those members. In addition, those members will be personally liable. In the example given in para. 3.81 above, if the Chairman did not have the requisite authority, he or she will be personally liable to pay and will not be able to claim an indemnity from the club's funds. On the other hand, provided that he acted within the scope of his or her authority, he/she will be entitled to an indemnity from the Club's funds.

Ratification

3.86 An unauthorised contract made by an agent may be ratified by the principal. But the contract may only be ratified by the person or persons on whose behalf the contract was made. To enable this to happen the principal(s) must know all the relevant circumstances. Ratification may also be inferred from silence or acquiescence.

3.87 This is a very difficult area, particularly if the committee takes decisions with which some of its members disagree strongly. The sorts of questions likely to be involved in controversial cases are:

• Did the members who took the decision have the authority to do so?

- Did they act within the scope of their authority?
- What is the position of those members who voted against the decision?
- If the decision was taken without authority was it later ratified?

Urgent and emergency decisions

3.88 It may help to show how these rules may work by looking at an example. The Chairman of the committee is alerted by the Secretary in confidence to problems with the accounts. It appears that the club's chief accountant may have been acting fraudulently. The Chairman asks the Secretary to conduct a confidential investigation; the outcome is that the Secretary confirms that there is strong evidence of fraud by the chief accountant. The Chairman approaches the club's lawyers for advice. Their advice is to dismiss the accountant immediately with an agreed pay-off, subject to the accountant signing a confidential settlement agreement. The Chairman invites the accountant to a meeting and asks him to consider the proposal; he is given a week to respond. Within the week, he signs the agreement, leaves the club and receives the agreed sum by way of compensation. At the next committee meeting the Chairman informs the members of what has happened. Some of the members express deep unhappiness at the decision arrived at.

3.89 The following questions arise here:

1. Did the Chairman have authority to act?
2. If so, what was the nature of his authority?
3. If he did not have any form of authority, is he personally liable on the settlement agreement?
4. May the committee ratify the agreement?
5. If it does by a majority, what is the position of (a) those who voted for ratification and (b) those who voted against?

3.90 The answers to the questions posed in the preceding paragraphs are as follows:

1. There is no evidence that the Chairman had actual authority.

2. So, if he had any form of authority, it would be apparent/ostensible authority.

3. If he had no authority, he would be personally liable on the settlement agreement unless it is ratified by the committee.

4. The committee may ratify the agreement, but their decision would not enable them to claim an indemnity from club funds *unless* they had informed themselves of all the material details of the agreement. Bearing in mind that it was confidential, they would probably have been unable to do so.

5. Those who voted for ratification would be exposed to a claim by the ex-employee if the agreed compensation was not paid out. Those who voted against would be able to seek an indemnity from the other members.

In practice – and assuming that the compensation was paid to the ex-employee – it is unlikely that the Chairman or any members of the committee would be exposed to a claim. But the example given shows the risks involved.

3.91 This type of problem was looked at in *Davies v Barnes Webster & Sons Ltd* (2011). The case involved the Romford and Gidea Park Rugby Club. Mr Davies was the president, a trustee and a member of the management committee of the club. At a special meeting the club membership (including Mr Davies) resolved to redevelop the clubhouse. That meant entering into a substantial contract with the builders, Barnes Webster. The contract was signed by the club's treasurer on behalf of the club. The builders claimed a further sum of £147,000 in respect of authorised variations of the contract. This sum was not paid, and Mr Davies was served with a demand for payment; he did not pay. The judge refused to set aside this demand and said:

"The basic position is that . . . members of an unincorporated association such as this club are not personally liable for the acts of those who enter into contracts in the course of the affairs of the club. Exactly who is liable depends on the constitution of the club and what acts of authority and ratification have occurred. It is possible for all the

members to be liable if they give appropriate authority, either in terms of the general rules of the club or in respect of particular transactions. But the general starting point is of course that that is not their intention. A member of a club is . . . not liable for more than his or her subscriptions or other regular dues."

The judge went on to say that the correct analysis of the problem before him was the proper application of the principles of agency and he stated:

". . . the management committee was entrusted with the development of the club and one would expect the management committee to be liable for the debts incurred by officers of the club and those dealing with it."

3.92 The *Davies* case did not deal with the position of the member who disagrees with the decision arrived at by the majority. This is a difficult area, mainly because there is little authority to give guidance. The old case of *Todd v Emly* (1841) (mentioned at para. 3.58, above) is commonly referred to for guidance in these sorts of situations. In that case, the judge suggested that, if members of a committee are acting together for a "common purpose", then each member of the committee has authority to bind the other members involved in the common purpose. If that is correct, that would mean that in most cases dissentient, absent or abstaining members could still be held liable. The answer to the question posed in para. 3.89 above is therefore likely to be that they would be liable even if they voted against the agreement.

Dealing with future problems

3.93 Assuming that the Chairman's actions are ratified, the committee and, in due course, the members of the club, need to give thought to how these kinds of situations may be handled in the future. There are two ways of doing this:

1.   The committee should examine its procedures to enable it to take urgent or emergency decisions speedily and without the need to convene a formal meeting. This may be done by

changing the rules to enable the committee to meet by telephone/video link/email.

2. The committee should examine whether express or actual authority should be given to anyone and, if so, to whom.

In the second situation, there is a further question: whether the authority given should be subject to any limitations.

3.94 Such problems as those examined above do not have easy solutions, but it is important that the committee should address them. As part of the examination of the conduct of committee meetings, it may be necessary to change the way committee meetings are handled. That will probably entail a change in the club's rules.

Liability of committee members

Introduction

3.95 This section follows on from what was said in the previous section. It proceeds on the assumption that personal liability against members of the committee is established. If that is so, then the question here is how best to protect them.

3.96 The first point to note is that the members of the club do not have any liability. The members' liability is to pay their subscription. Assuming that it has been paid, then they cannot be made liable for any expenditure which has been authorised by the committee and which is not paid for.

3.97 That being so, the following are possible solutions to the question of protection of the committee members:

1. raising the members' subscriptions;
2. indemnity; and
3. insurance.

Raising subscriptions

3.98 Raising subscriptions is a common method of dealing with a shortfall in funds when a club needs to finance a large project. It would be perfectly in order to call a general meeting either to raise subscriptions generally or to have a one-off rise in subscriptions or to make a levy on members. The club might also consider – again by means of a general meeting – establishing a reserve or sinking fund to help in the financing of future projects.

Indemnity

3.99 There is nothing to prevent the club having a rule providing for committee members to be indemnified out of club funds for expenditure incurred in the proper discharge of their duties. A blanket indemnity would be unwise, but a more restricted rule indemnifying members of the committee, officers of the club and officials of the club out of club funds against any legal claim made against them in connection with the proper discharge of their duties.

3.100 An example of an indemnity rule is:

"The members of the Committee of the Club shall be entitled to be indemnified by the Club out of club funds in the event of any legal or monetary claim made against them by third parties in connection with the proper discharge of their duties."

Insurance

3.101 The club should give consideration to taking out insurance in relation to the activities of the committee members, if it does not already have insurance. Insurance would not only cover the activities of the committee members but also the activities of its employees. In the absence of insurance, the club would be liable for negligent acts committed by its employees. See para. 4.35 for a discussion of this matter.

Meetings

3.102 The holding of meetings is an essential part of the operation of the club, since they are the means by which the members control the way the club is run. In the very unlikely event that the rules did not make any provision for meetings to be held, a rule would undoubtedly be implied entitling the members to convene and hold meetings. But it is clearly desirable that the rules should provide for meetings *expressly*.

3.103 Two types of meetings may be held:

- The Annual General Meeting; and
- Special Meetings

In addition, the club may also from time to time hold informal meetings for discussing matters which are relevant to the operation of the club. For example, a residential club may be working on proposals for refurbishing the bedroom accommodation and wish to sound out the members' views. It is not necessary to go through the formalities for calling a meeting unless a resolution is proposed which would be binding on all the members. At that point, the formalities of a general meeting are required.

3.104 Special meetings of the club are meetings which deal with special business. They are called for a particular and stated purpose or purposes which cannot be dealt with at an AGM. The only business which can be transacted at such a meeting is the business for which the meeting was called. They are usually called Extraordinary General Meetings (EGMs); their correct legal name is a "special general meeting". They are discussed at para. 3.140 below.

Annual General Meeting

3.105 The Annual General Meeting (AGM) is the opportunity for the members to receive reports upon what has happened during the previous year. The main items of business are:

- Receiving reports from the Treasurer and Secretary
- Receiving and (if thought fit) approving the club's accounts
- Electing the officers of the club and the members of the committee
- Fixing the subscriptions; and
- Transacting the *general* business of the club.

The date of the AGM is usually fixed in the rules by specifying date before which the meeting must be held. The conduct of the meeting is considered below: see para. 3.120.

3.106 In this section, the following matters are considered:

- notice of the meeting;
- agenda;
- attendance and quorum;
- chairing of the meeting;
- motions;
- voting; and
- minutes.

Notice of the meeting

3.107 It is important that the correct notice of a meeting should be given. This means that:

1. the notice should be given within the correct time-frame; and
2. the notice must be given to every member who is entitled to attend and vote.

The notice should set out the date, the time, the place and the nature of the business to be conducted or transacted.

Length of notice

3.108 The rules should specify the length of notice to be given in respect of any particular type of meeting. The normal period may be as little as 14 days, but it is usually 21 for AGMs and EGMs. A failure to give the correct notice will mean that the meeting has been incorrectly convened. Any resolution passed at such a meeting will therefore be invalid. An example is the case of *Labouchère v Earl of Wharncliffe* (1879), which involved the Beefsteak Club. A meeting was called to discuss the expulsion of Mr Labouchère. The rules of the club required a fortnight's notice of the meeting. At the meeting the committee considered a resolution to expel him, which was carried. The notice of the meeting was posted on 1 November and the meeting was held on 14 November. The judge held that the meeting has been irregularly called and, therefore, that the resolution to expel was invalid. (This case was also discussed at para. 3.40 above.)

3.109 This means that great care must be taken over notices. Clearly, the first consideration is the giving of the correct time. The calculation of the time period has given rise to many disputes, as is clear from the number of cases in this area. Much depends on the wording of the rule in dispute. In *Labouchère*, the rules required a fortnight's notice. In cases like that – or where 14 days' notice is specified – the day of service of the notice is excluded. So, the meeting called by the Beefsteak Club would have been valid had it been called on 31 October or had the notice been given on 1 November for the meeting to be held on 15 November. On the other hand, if the rules state that the period of time begins with a specified date, the first day is included. In the case of rules which specify "14 clear days", "not less than 14 days" or "at least 14 days", the last day as well as the first day is not taken into account. In the example already discussed, that would mean that the meeting could not be held until 16 November if notice were given on 1 November. Clearly, this is an area where care needs to be taken.

Communication of notice to members

3.110 The starting point here is the rules. They may specify various forms of communication – for example, posting the notice in the club house and communication by post. Nowadays, with the advent of the internet and electronic communication, communication is likely to be by email. This has been made possible by the Electronic Communications Act 2000. It is important for the rules to cover all these methods of communication. This is because, if they do not, a meeting called by a notice which is not permitted by the rules will risk being held by a court to be invalid. It is important, however, that the rules *do not exclude* non-electronic methods of communication. If they did, they would, in effect, be confining the membership of the club to those who owned a computer.

3.111 There is always the risk that, whatever method of communication is used, a member may not have received the notice. There are two ways of dealing with this:

1. to include a rule which states that the notice is deemed to have been received within a specified time of it being sent or delivered (depending on the method used); and/or

2. to stipulate that the accidental omission to give notice to one or more members will not invalidate the meeting.

3.112 For example, the club's rules may say something like:

"All notices in writing required to be given by the Club to the members under these rules may be sent by post and/or by electronic means. This shall include notices posted on the club's website. All notices sent to members at their notified address, whichever means of communication are used, shall be deemed to have arrived two days after dispatch by the Club unless the contrary is shown. If any notice sent by the Club does not arrive or arrives late at the address of the member that shall not invalidate the meeting. Similarly, the accidental omission to give due notice of the meeting to one or more members shall not invalidate the meeting."

Agenda

3.113 The items on the agenda of an AGM are usually the following:

- To receive apologies for absence
- To approve the Minutes of the previous AGM
- Matters arising
- To receive a report from the Secretary on the club's activities since the previous AGM
- To receive a report from the Treasurer and, if considered fit, to approve the club's accounts for the previous financial year
- To elect the club's Officers and members of the Committee, and also to appoint the Honorary Auditor
- To fix subscriptions
- Any other business.

3.114 The final item on the Agenda – any other business or AOB – merits consideration. Its use at an AGM is to deal with matters arising out of the general business of the club, that is the preceding items on the agenda. The AOB item cannot be used to pass a specific proposal or to raise matters which are not connected with the general business of the club. In the event of a dispute as to whether a matter raised as AOB is proper it is for the Chairman of the meeting to decide. In addition, the agenda may stipulate that any member who wishes to raise a matter of general business at the AGM must give written notice to the Secretary by a specified date before the AGM. If that is not done, the member will not be allowed to proceed.

Attendance and quorum

3.115 Since a meeting is a private meeting of the club members it follows that strangers (including members of the press) do not have a right to attend meetings of the club. The behaviour of members at the meeting is dealt with below: see para. 3.124.

Quorum

3.116 It is crucial that the meeting is attended by a quorum of members. A quorum is the number of members who must be present at the meeting for it to be a valid meeting. The rules should specify the quorum necessary for a general meeting (and also for meetings such as committee meetings: see para. 3.46). It is up to the club to specify a quorum but good practice would suggest that it should not be too small. This would avoid control being taken by a small clique of members. The size of the quorum clearly depends on the number of members. If the club has, say, 1000 members, then it would be appropriate to specify a quorum of 50 (5% of the membership). But there is nothing to preclude a higher quorum being specified. The risk is that, if too large a number were specified, the meetings would risk inquoracy. For the meeting to be validly constituted it is not necessary that all the members are physically present in one room, provided that proper aids are used to enable members in overflow rooms to participate. This has become increasingly common in recent years, with electronic aids such as 'Zoom'.

3.117 The other question here is whether a meeting should be quorate at all times or only at the beginning. It is clear that it should be. However, a member who left the meeting deliberately so as to make it inquorate could not rely on the lack of quorum to argue that the proceedings were invalid after his or her departure.

Lack of quorum

3.118 The rules also need to deal with the situation where the quorum is not met at the start of the meeting. They should state whether a period of grace is to be allowed. If they do not, then it would still be within the Chairman's powers to delay the start of the meeting for 30 minutes to allow for the entry of latecomers.

Electronic meetings

3.119 An example of a rule which might be included in the club's rules is:

1. *"This rule supplements Rules ** and **. [Rules relating to the holding of the club's meetings]*

2. *The Committee shall have the power in appropriate cases to hold and conduct a general meeting in such a way that members who are not present together at the same place may by electronic means attend and speak and vote at it.*

3. *Any proposed written resolution by the Committee or a member must be circulated to every member who is entitled to vote at the electronic meeting at least 21 days before this meeting. The resolution may be circulated by post, by email or by publishing it on the Club's website".*

Chairing and conduct of the meeting

3.120 The duties of the chairman of the meeting are important. He or she must make sure that the meeting is orderly and that its business is properly transacted. It has been said that the Chairman's overall duty is "to act not as dictator but as a servant of the members of the body, according to law." (See *John v Rees* (1970).) The Chairman has a duty of impartiality and should stand down in the event of having a personal interest in the outcome of any motion.

3.121 At the start of the meeting, the Chairman needs to make sure that it has been properly convened (see para. 3.107, above) and that it is quorate (see para. 3.116, above). During the meeting, his or her obligations are:

- to make sure that the agenda is followed;

- to make sure that all the items of business are duly considered and, if necessary, voted on; and
- to rule on any points of order which may be raised.

3.122 In addition, the other duties of the Chairman are:

- not to alter the order of the agenda unless a majority of the meeting agrees to this course;
- not to introduce a motion of his own which is not on the agenda;
- to deal with amendments to motions in the correct order;
- to arrange for the precise motion which is being put to the meeting to be read out and voted on; and
- to make sure that voting procedures are conducted properly.

In general, the Chairman should conduct proceedings with the agreement of the meeting, bearing in mind, though, that he is in charge of it.

3.123 It is not unknown for a meeting to descend into disorder. If that happens, then the Chairman should first try to restore order. If order cannot be restored, then the Chairman should adjourn the meeting briefly. A decision to adjourn the meeting must be made with the agreement of those present, since normally the power of adjournment rests with the meeting.

3.124 The case of *John v Rees* (1970) is important in this context, since it contains a detailed discussion of dealing with disorderly meetings and the Chairman's power of adjournment. The case involved a political meeting which descended into chaos. The Chairman of the meeting took various steps, one of which was to adjourn the meeting *indefinitely*. After that, he left the meeting. The judge held that the adjournment was invalid and, therefore, that it was permissible to continue the meeting with another person chairing it. The judge said this about the duties of the Chairman when dealing with disorderly meetings:

> *"The first duty of the chairman of a meeting is to keep order if he can.*
> *If there is disorder, his duty . . . is to make earnest and sustained efforts*

to restore order, and for this purpose to summon to his aid any officers or others whose assistance is available. If all his efforts are in vain, he should endeavour to put into operation whatever provisions for adjournment there are in the rules, as by obtaining a resolution to adjourn. If this proves impossible, he should exercise his inherent power to adjourn the meeting for a short while, such as 15 minutes, taking due steps to ensure so far as possible that all present know of this adjournment."

He then went on to discuss what limitations there are on the exercise of the power of adjournment and continued:

"First, . . . the power and duty must be exercised bona fide for the purpose of forwarding and facilitating the meeting, and not for the purpose of interruption or procrastination. Second, . . . the adjournment must be for no longer than the necessities appear to dictate. If the adjournment is merely for such period as the chairman considers to be reasonably necessary for the restoration of order, it would be within his power and his duty; a longer adjournment would not. One must remember that to attend a meeting may for some mean travelling far and giving up much leisure. An adjournment to another day when a mere 15 minutes might suffice to restore order may well impose an unjustifiable burden on many; for they must either once more travel far and give up their leisure, or else remain away and lose their chance to speak and vote at the meeting."

Motions

3.125 A motion is a proposal. If it is approved by the meeting it becomes a resolution. At this point, the members have decided to act in accordance with the proposal, as agreed. Problems may arise is where amendments are proposed. Unless they are properly handled, the meeting may become chaotic.

3.126 Normally, the original motion and any proposed amendments will be set out on the agenda. It is up to the Chairman to decide upon the order for dealing with the proposed amendments. Members may also orally propose amendments from the floor, but they must be within the scope of the motion and not merely a disagreement with the original motion. The effect of the proposed amendment should also be reasonably clear. It is normal – but not necessary – for the chairman to ask for a seconder for the motion. The amendment is then discussed and put to the vote. If successful, the amended motion becomes the motion before the meeting and may be itself be amended. If the proposed amendment is unsuccessful, the original motion continues to be discussed. The decision whether or not to accept an amendment may be made by a simple majority.

Voting

3.127 The three most common methods of voting used in club meetings are:

- show of hands;
- poll; and
- ballot.

If the chairman of the meeting senses that the mood of the meeting does not require a vote, then he or she may decide to proceed without one. This is known as "acclamation".

3.128 It is becoming common to use electronic media for the conduct of meetings. This enables members to attend either physically or by means of electronic aids such as Zoom. Any meeting is likely to have members attending by a combination of the two methods. Arrangements therefore need to be made for the meeting to use electronic means for voting, as well as the traditional methods.

Show of hands

3.129 This is usually the first method of voting at a meeting. If the meeting is large, then it is advisable to appoint scrutineers to count the votes.

3.130 The procedure adopted here depends on the rules. If the rules stipulate that the first method of voting must be show of hands, then the chairman must first proceed with a show of hands. If there is no such rule, then the chairman may proceed to a poll without first calling for a show of hands. Similarly, a member who is dissatisfied with the result of a show of hands may demand a poll as of right, unless there is a rule to the contrary. If there is a valid request for a poll, then the result of any vote by show of hands is of no effect.

Poll

3.131 A poll is a more accurate means of establishing the true vote of the meeting, since it openly records the number of votes. The members either sign an individual voting slip or a voting list. If a poll is taken, this gives rise to the question as to whether it is restricted to those present at the meeting or is open to all the members of the club. It has long been established that the poll may be restricted to those present at the meeting: see *R v Rector of St Mary, Lambeth* (1838).

Ballot

3.132 This aspect of voting gives rise to a number of issues:

- equality of voting rights;
- use of proxies; and
- requisite majority.

3.133 The Equality Act 2010 requires that all members of the club must have equal voting rights: see s. 101(2). This means that, for example, a club may not give greater voting rights to its male members than to its female members.

3.134 A proxy is someone appointed by a member to exercise all or some of his or her rights in relation to the meeting. If proxies are to be allowed, then the rules need to make specific provision for them. If a poll is called, then a proxy may vote on behalf of as many members as he or she is proxy for. It is normal practice to send out proxy forms with the notice of the meeting.

3.135 The rules of the club should make clear what majority is required for any resolution of the members to be binding on the entire membership. As a general rule, a simple majority is all that is required. But the rules may stipulate a different voting majority for different types of resolution. So, for example, it is normal to require a two-thirds majority for more important and far-reaching resolutions, for example, a resolution to change the rules of the club.

3.136 Finally, it should be noted that it is normal to give the chairman of the meeting a casting vote in addition to his or her ordinary vote.

Minutes

3.137 The purpose of having minutes of a meeting is to provide a "fair and accurate record" of what has been decided at a meeting. This should avoid arguments at a later stage when recollections have faded. The point of the minutes is not to record all that was said at the meeting. Rather, their point is to provide a concise summary of the meeting.

3.138 This means that they should record the essential elements of the discussion and should provide the full text of any resolution which was adopted. What is important is that anyone reading the minutes after the event would be able to understand what had happened. It adds nothing to the minutes to add surplus description to what was said. So, it is unnecessary to record the emotions with which any statement was made. The fact that the maker of the statement took a particular position in relation to the matter in hand should be recorded in his or her vote. If there is a dispute about how a member's views should be recorded, the chairman should be asked to make a ruling.

3.139 The chairman should sign the minutes of the previous meeting once the members who attended the previous meeting have approved their accuracy. If the minutes need to be corrected in any way, an additional minute correcting the mistake should be added and signed.

Extraordinary General Meetings

3.140 These meetings are special meetings of the club which deal with special business. They are called for a particular and stated purpose or purposes which cannot be dealt with at an AGM. The only business which can be transacted at such a meeting is the business for which the meeting was called. They are usually called

Extraordinary General Meetings (EGMs); their correct legal name is a "special general meeting".

3.141 As a general rule, EGMs may be called either by order of the committee or by a requisition signed by a specified minimum number of members. The rules need to make specific provision for the following matters:

- the minimum number of members needed to sign a requisition;
- whether the requisition should be in writing;
- the amount of notice of the meeting required to be given;
- the requirements relating to the motion to be debated at the meeting; and
- the voting requirements in relation to the proposed motion(s).

3.142 Although the requisition might be oral, it is sensible for the rules to require it to be in writing. If the committee refused to convene an EGM on the requisition of the specified minimum number of members, then the requisitioning members could probably convene the meeting, though there is no direct legal authority relating to this point.

3.143 A normal period of notice for an EGM is either 21 or 28 days. It is possible, though, for the rules to provide for the committee to shorten the notice, for example to seven days, in exceptional circumstances. This might be necessary if the club ran into a serious financial crisis.

3.144 Since the purpose of an EGM is to discuss the specific business for which the meeting has been called, the rules should set out the time limits for delivery of the notice of the motion. So, for example, the rules may require the requisitioners to give notice of the motion to be discussed at the EGM as the same time as they give notice of the meeting itself. As a precaution, the rules might add something like the following:

"At an extraordinary general meeting, a motion may be debated and decided only if notice has been given in accordance with Rule **, and, except where the motion is proposed by the General Committee, the

motion is proposed and seconded at the meeting by members with the power to vote."

3.145 So far as the voting requirements are concerned, the rules should stipulate:

- the number of members required to be present at the meeting;
- the number of votes in favour of the motion for it to be carried; and
- the number of votes in favour as a percentage of members present.

For example, the rules might stipulate that a motion will not be carried unless:

(a) at least 75 members with the power to vote are present;

(b) the numbers voting in favour must be not less than 50; and

(c) that number must comprise no less than two thirds of the members present and voting.

4. The Club and Third Parties

Introduction

4.1 This chapter looks at the club's dealings with third parties – whether they are employees of the club or contractors engaged to do work on the club's premises – and, particularly, the consequences of those dealings going wrong. In that event, there will be a question of liability. That, in turn, leads to the question – already considered in Chapter 3 – who in the club is liable. This chapter, therefore, is closely linked with the discussion in Chapter 3. The issues considered here are more likely to affect larger clubs which own or lease premises. Small clubs with no premises are less likely to be affected. Occasions may arise, however, when they too are involved with third parties, usually in the context of commercial contracts.

4.2 The focus of this chapter is, therefore, on liability. Liability may arise in a number of different situations and from a number of different causes. These are examined below. There are two types of liability:

1. "primary" liability; and
2. "vicarious" liability.

Primary liability arises where someone does something themselves and, because of a breach of some sort, they are liable to pay for the breach.

Vicarious liability arises where a person is liable for the behaviour of someone else. In the context of a club, vicarious liability is most likely to arise because it employs staff and a member of the staff commits an act which gives rise to liability. In that situation, the club will be said to be vicariously liable for the act of its employee arising from its status as an employer. That means that it will be liable to compensate the victim of the act committed by its member of staff.

4.3   Some actions taken by the club may be actions which incur primary liability, for example entering into contracts with third parties. Other actions may be actions for which the club is vicariously liable because of the fact that it is an employer. Both types of liability are looked at below.

4.4   The rest of the chapter will look at the types of liability which are most likely to arise. These are:

- contractual liability;
- tortious liability;
- liability as a landlord or tenant;
- liability in relation to employees, particularly under the Equality Act 2010;
- health and safety; and
- criminal liability.

4.5   *Contractual liability* is likely to arise in relation to the club's dealings with a range of outside contractors – ranging from suppliers of food and beverages, on the one hand, to contractors who do work on the club's premises, on the other. Employment contracts are also within this category.

4.6   *Tortious liability* arises under the law of tort. A tort is usually defined as a civil wrong. What this means is that a person (A) does something which affects someone else (B). The act done by A is not a criminal act but results in harm or damage to B or B's property. B's remedy is to sue A in the civil courts (County Court or High Court) for compensation. This is known as "damages". The main examples of this type of liability are liability in negligence, liability under the Occupiers' Liability Act 1957 and nuisance. These are explained further below.

4.7   *Liability as a landlord or tenant* is most likely to occur if the club leases its premises from a landlord. The question most likely to arise here will be in relation to the club's position as a tenant. It is unlikely to own premises and lease them out as a landlord.

4.8   *Liability in relation to employees* is likely to arise in relation to matters falling within the relevant Employment legislation. The Acts most likely to apply are the Employment Relations Act 1996 and the Equality Act 2010. The 1996 Act contains provisions relating to a number of statutory rights. These include:

- maternity leave and parental leave;
- rights in relation to flexible working; and
- rights in relation to termination of employment, including the right not to be unfairly dismissed

The Equality Act 2010 deals with matters relating to alleged unlawful discrimination. Liability under the Act may arise in relation to two main categories:

1. members, associate members and guests; and
2. employees.

Draft legislation is before Parliament relating to employment rights. Its effect – once enacted – will be to enhance employees' rights under the 1996 Act.

4.9 *Health and Safety* As an employer, the club has obligations under the Health and Safety at Work Act 1974 (as amended) and numerous regulations published in connection with it. Breaches of the Act may lead to prosecution.

4.10 *Criminal liability* may also arise in a variety of different ways. The most obvious areas – particularly in relation to premises which serve food and beverages are:

1. sale of alcohol;
2. food safety; and
3. smoking.

4.11 Liability may also arise because of breaches of legislation affecting property and substances which escape from the property. So, for example, a club may be liable to prosecution for a breach of the Water Resources Act 1991 or for the legislation relating to Tree Preservation Orders. See para. 4.98 below.

Primary liability

4.12 Primary liability arises where someone has a duty which they fail to perform. It may help to consider a number of examples here:

1. A enters into a contract to sell goods to B and does not honour the contract. This may be because the goods are defective or because he or she does not deliver them at all. A is said to be in breach of contract and will be liable to compensate B for the breach.

2. C is the owner of premises. The steps to the entrance are damaged. D goes up the steps and, because of the damage, slips and breaks a leg. C should have repaired the steps. C will therefore be liable to D for negligence (a type of tort). He or she will also be liable under the Occupiers' Liability Act 1957 because of the failure to repair the steps.

3. E is the tenant of premises. The lease under which the premises are held contains various covenants which E does not honour. He or she is therefore in breach of the lease.

4. F is an employer. F commits an unlawful act of race discrimination against G, an unlawful act of sex discrimination against H and dismisses L.

5. M is the owner of a golf course. A leakage of oil from the club's storage tank occurs; the leakage pollutes a nearby watercourse. M is prosecuted. (See para. 4.98 below)

4.13 The examples above are all examples of primary liability. This type of liability arises where A has an obligation and breaks it.

4.14 In the context of a club is it easy to see how the club may incur liability of the sorts outlined above. So, if, for example, the club contracts with a decorator to refurbish the club's premises, it has incurred contractual liability. If it does not pay the decorator's bill when presented it will be liable for breach of contract.

4.15 So too, if the club's premises are in some way defective and a member suffers injury as a result of the defect, the club may be liable for negligence and for breach of the Occupiers' Liability Act 1957.

Vicarious liability

4.16 A person may also incur liability in a situation where the act complained of is not done by A but by B. B is A's employee. In that situation, A is said to be "vicariously liable" for the acts of B. Smaller clubs may well not have employees. But a club of any size is likely to have them. Vicarious liability only arises in relation to *employees*. An employer is not vicariously liable for others whose services it uses if they are not employees: see para. 4.23 below.

4.17 As with the discussion of primary liability, it may help to give some examples of situations in which vicarious liability may arise. Some of these examples follow on from what was said above.

1. The club employs B as a handyman. B carries out a repair negligently and, as a result, a club member suffers an injury and a visitor also suffers injuries. The club may find itself sued by the member and the visitor for negligence and for breach of the Occupiers' Liability Act 1957.

2. The club is large and employs a secretary (C) to manage its affairs. C commits the following acts:
    a) C commits an act of race discrimination against D;
    b) C also commits an act of sex discrimination against E;
    c) C dismisses F, a long-serving employee.

3. The club is a golf club. It owns a golf course with a number of trees on it subject to Tree Preservation Orders. The club's secretary (C) arranges for a number of the trees to be felled. This is in breach of the Orders.

4.18 Vicarious liability may arise in two ways:

1. where a tort is committed; or
2. by virtue of legislation.

In the first case, above, the law says that an employer is vicariously liable for the actions of its employees. This is called vicarious liability "at common law".

In relation to the second type of vicarious liability, the relevant legislation here is the Equality Act 2010. The Act imposes its own type of vicarious liability for acts of discrimination which are made unlawful by the Act. It is different from common law vicarious liability and is called statutory vicarious liability. It is considered at para. 4.24 below.

4.19 In the examples given in para. 4.17 above, the club would be vicariously liable at common law for the acts committed in example 1. In the case of example 2, it would be vicariously liable under the 2010 Act for the unlawful acts of sex and race discrimination. In the case of example 3, the club's secretary, its officers and the club would be liable to prosecution. The club secretary authorised the felling, and the officers gave instructions for the trees to be felled. They would all be liable to prosecution. The club (in practice, its committee) would be vicariously liable for the actions of C and the officers.

4.20 *Common law vicarious liability* means that the employer is made answerable in law for the acts of the employee. It is not necessary to show that the employer was in any way to blame for what happened. It arises because of the relationship of employer/employee. An employer who employs an employee in effect has to pay for any acts of negligence committed by the employee. The test is whether the act committed by the employee was done *in the course of employment*.

4.21 In the context of a club this rule means that the members of the committee will be vicariously liable for the acts of the employee. The question to be asked is: was the action of the employee "so closely connected" with what the employer authorised or expected of the employee in the performance of his employment that it would be fair and just to conclude that the employer is vicariously liable for the damage sustained by the victim as a result of the employee's act? This test was set out by the Court of Appeal in *Mattis v Pollock (t/a Flamingo's Nightclub)*. In that case a club owner was held vicariously liable for acts of assault committed by the club doorman on a visitor to the nightclub.

4.22 Not all those employed to do work on a club's premises are employees of the club. Instead of using employees to do work on the club's premises the committee may use workers who are not employees to carry it out. They are called "independent contractors". The general rule is that if a person employs an independent contractor to do work, that person is not liable for any tort committed by the contractor or by the contractor's employees in the course of carrying out that work.

4.23 If a question of vicarious liability arises it will be necessary to establish whether the person who committed the act was an employee or an independent contractor. This question is not always easy to answer but the starting point for the discussion is the question posed by the court in *Ready Mixed Concrete (South East) v Minister of Pensions and Social Security* (1968): "Is the worker in business on his own account?" To answer that question all the relevant factors need to be considered.

4.24 *Statutory vicarious liability* under the Equality Act 2010 is imposed by section 109. This says:

(1) "Anything done by a person (A) in the course of A's employment must be treated as also done by the employer.

(2) . . .

(3) It does not matter whether that thing is done with the employer's . . . knowledge or approval.

(4) In proceedings against A's employer (B) in respect of anything alleged to have been done by A in the course of A's employment it is a defence for B to show that B took all reasonable steps to prevent A—

(a)   from doing that thing, or

(b)   from doing anything of that description."

4.25 The difference between the two types of vicarious liability is that an employer has a defence to vicarious liability under the Act if it can show that it took all reasonable steps to prevent the employee from committing the act of discrimination. In practice, this means that the employer needs to provide training for its employees so that they are aware of the requirements of the Act. If the defence is available to it, then it will not be liable for the act of discrimination. The employee will remain liable, though.

Contractual liability

4.26 A club is likely to incur contractual liability in relation to two types of contract:

1. Commercial contracts; and
2. Employment contracts.

Commercial contracts

4.27 The commercial contracts entered into by the club will depend on the nature of the club. A club with premises (whether owned freehold or under a lease) will probably have a bar and possibly a restaurant; it may also have bedrooms. So, it will enter into contracts relating to the provision of food and beverages, and contracts for the maintenance of the premises. A club without its own premises is less likely to enter into commercial contracts, but it too may need to enter into contracts with third parties. For example, a sports club which does not have its own premises may need to hire storage facilities to store its equipment or it may wish to employ coaches for its members; an arts club may need to hire premises for its meetings and engage speakers to speak at those meetings.

Employment contracts

4.28 Much the same is true in relation to employment contracts. A club with premises will need to employ staff; that will involve entering into contracts of employment with them. In addition to issues arising from their contracts of employment, the staff will enjoy statutory rights under the Employment Rights Act 1996, including the statutory right not to be unfairly dismissed. These are considered at para. 4.58, below.

4.29 The termination of the employment contracts of the staff is unlikely to lead to breach of contract claims. It is more likely to lead to claims that their statutory rights in relation to dismissal have been breached. This is because, in relation to most of the staff, the level of pay and the length of notice entitlement are such that they are best advised to claim unfair dismissal under the 1996 Act. If the club employs a secretary, however, the dismissal of the secretary may lead to a claim for breach of contract (also known as "wrongful dismissal"), in addition to his or her statutory right of unfair dismissal. This will be because he or she is likely to have a high level of salary and entitlement to a lengthy period of notice (for example, 3 or 6 months).

4.30 Whether a dismissed employee claims unfair or wrongful dismissal depends on a number of factors. As a general rule, an employee with a fairly high salary and a long notice entitlement will be more likely to sue for wrongful dismissal/breach of contract in the County Court or High Court. It is also possible to pursue an unfair dismissal claim at the same time but there will be offsets between the compensation awarded in both claims.

4.31 An employee who is entitled to one month's notice, for example, and is not highly paid is more likely to make a claim in an employment tribunal.

Tortious liability

4.32 A tort is usually defined as a civil wrong. It does not arise from a contract but gives rise to an action for damages (compensation) in the civil courts. The torts most likely to affect a club are the torts of negligence and nuisance. There is also the possibility of a claim under the Occupiers' Liability Act 1957, which is similar to a claim for negligence.

4.33 The situations which give rise to tortious liability involve actions which affect third parties. These may be people who are not members of the club, though in some cases members or employees of the club may also be affected by a tort. As with contractual liability, tortious liability is most likely to arise where the club has premises. Any claim is likely to arise in connection with activities on the premises.

4.34 In the case of clubs which have premises where sports are played, there are additional risks of liability. These may arise in relation to injuries suffered by spectators at sporting events and injuries suffered by those involved in playing sport. This last group is discussed at para. 4.46 below.

Negligence

4.35 The tort of negligence was established by the case of *Donoghue v Stevenson* (1932). The case involved a customer of a café who drank a bottle of ginger beer which contained the remains of a decomposed snail and who, as a result, suffered illness. Lord Atkin said this:

> *"You must take reasonable care to avoid acts or omissions which you can reasonably foresee would be likely to injure your neighbour. Who, then, in law is my neighbour? The answer seems to be — persons who are so closely and directly affected by my act that I ought reasonably to have them in contemplation as being so affected when I am directing my mind to the acts or omissions which are called in question."*

4.36 The point about the case was that the victim was someone who was affected by the negligent manufacture of the ginger beer. The café which sold the drink was not to blame for the negligent manufacture and so could not have been sued for breach of contract. The manufacturer had no contract with the consumer and a breach of contract case brought by the consumer would have failed. So, to follow Lord Atkin's words, the person who drank the ginger beer was a person who was closely and directly affected by the act of the manufacturer which ought to have had the consumer in contemplation when it manufactured the drink. In other words, the manufacturer had a duty of care to the consumer.

4.37 The principles established by this case relate to what are known as of proximity and foreseeability. In other words, they relate to whether the victim of the event is sufficiently proximate to be classed as a "neighbour" (using Lord Atkins's word) and whether it was reasonably foreseeable that the accident might happen. In addition to satisfying itself that those two principles have been established, the court also needs to be satisfied that the imposition of a duty of care on the person alleged to be responsible for the act of negligence is fair, just and reasonable.

4.38 This tort is the most likely to affect a club with premises which are not properly maintained or sports clubs where activities like cricket or golf take place. If someone suffers an injury because the premises have not been properly maintained, they will be able to sue the club for negligence. So too, sports clubs may find themselves sued for negligence, since their activities are likely to affect outsiders. This is an area of the law which has given rise to a large number of cases and a large volume of literature. Many of the cases involved claims for both negligence and nuisance. Some examples are:

- cases where cricket balls were hit by batsmen from a cricket ground into the gardens of neighbouring landowners or onto a neighbouring highway;
- cases where golf balls were hit from a golf course and injured motorists on a neighbouring road; and
- cases involving noise.

4.39 In the case of clubs on who have premises sports are played, there is the additional risk that a spectator watching a sporting activity taking place may be affected by that activity. In one case, a spectator was injured at a racetrack when a car somersaulted off the track and fell into the spectators' enclosure and injured him. In another, a spectator was injured by a horse which careered off the racecourse and knocked him down. The rider was a horseman of experience and skill. In both cases, the claims of the injured spectator failed. See *Hall v Brooklands Racing Club* (1933) and *Woolridge v Sumner* (1963).

4.40 A final point to note here is that a person who makes a claim based on the negligence of the club may find the amount of compensation reduced if they are held by the court to have contributed to their injury. This is known as "contributory negligence". It comes into play when the claimant is found to have failed to take reasonable care for his or her own well-being or safety and thus to have contributed to the injury caused because of the club's negligence. In this kind of case, the amount of compensation awarded will be reduced by the percentage of contributory negligence decided upon by the judge.

Occupier's liability

4.41 This type of liability arises by virtue of the Occupiers' Liability Act 1957. Section 2 of the Act introduces the idea of a 'common duty of care'. It states:

> "(1) An occupier of premises owes the same duty, the "common duty of care", to all his visitors, except in so far as he is free to and does extend, restrict, modify or exclude his duty to any visitor or visitors by agreement or otherwise.
>
> (2) The common duty of care is a duty to take such care as in all the circumstances of the case is reasonable to see that the visitor will be reasonably safe in using the premises for the purposes for which he is invited or permitted by the occupier to be there."

Section 2(1) makes it clear that an occupier may exclude or restrict liability to visitors "by agreement or otherwise".

4.42 The two main questions to arise are:

1. Who is an occupier? and
2. Who is a visitor?

So far as the first question is concerned, liability under the Act is most likely to affect a club which has premises, whether it owns them or leases them. If it hires out the premises to a third party for a particular event, then it would remain the occupier for the purposes of the Act. It could, however, exclude or restrict its liability by including a disclaimer clause in the contract with the third party. In the event of liability arising, then the members of the committee would be liable, since they would be treated as the occupiers for the purpose of the Act.

4.43 The duty of care under the Act is owed to visitors. A visitor is someone who is on the club's premises either because he or she has been invited onto the premises or because he or she has permission to be there. Someone who is there without an invitation or permission is treated by the law as a trespasser. Under the ordinary rules of negligence, a trespasser enters someone else's property at their own risk. But this rule no longer applies. The Occupiers' Liability Act 1984 was passed to provide for a limited statutory duty of care to trespassers. Section 1(3) of the Act states:

"An occupier of premises owes a duty to another (not being his visitor) in respect of any such risk as is referred to in subsection (1) above if —

(a) *he is aware of the danger or has reasonable grounds to believe that such a danger exists;*

(b) *he knows or has reasonable grounds to believe that the other is in the vicinity of the danger concerned or that he may come into the vicinity of the danger (in either case, whether the other has lawful authority for being in that vicinity or not); and*

(c) *the risk is one against which, in all the circumstances of the case, he may reasonably be expected to offer the other some protection."*

Nuisance

4.44 The tort of nuisance comes into play when the activities of an occupier of land affect the rights in or enjoyment of land enjoyed by someone else. There must be an escape from the occupier's land to the claimant's land. The liability may arise because of noise on the land which affects those nearby or because an object is hit from the land onto neighbouring land and causes an injury. Cases of this sort are most likely to affect clubs which exist to pursue sporting activities and tend to arise from injuries caused by golf balls being hit from a golf course or cricket balls being hit from a cricket ground onto neighbouring land or a nearby road. Other cases have involved noise coming from racing boats on a lake or caused by go-kart racing.

4.45 It is impossible to give clear guidance, since the cases themselves do not do so. It is important, however, that a club involved in sports such as those mentioned above is aware of the potential problems and takes out appropriate insurance.

Sports injuries

4.46 This matter is dealt with separately, since it may concern clubs which involve contact sports in which there is a higher risk of injury. The most obvious example of such a sport is rugby football, which has given rise to a number of cases. A player who is injured and wishes to sue is likely to sue the following:

- the referee;
- the club; and
- the professional association.

The case against the *referee* will be based on the argument that he/she failed to carry out their functions properly or committed errors of judgement. The case against the *professional association* will be on the basis that it is vicariously liable for the acts of the referee it appointed. The case against the *club* will be based on its failure to ensure that the referee or umpire was properly trained or appointed and its failure to carry out its duty of care towards players, spectators and – in the case of sports such as cricket or golf – neighbours.

4.47 This is an area where a club needs to ensure that the risk of the danger of injury is kept to a minimum and should give serious thought to taking out insurance.

Landlord and tenant relationships

Introduction

4.48 A club which needs premises for its activities will either own the premises outright (in other words, it owns the freehold) or it will have a lease. If it has a lease, it is said to have a leasehold of the premises. These are the only possible methods of owning land. In the case of a lease, it may be long or short but it creates an interest in land for a fixed period of time. By contrast, the *ownership* of land is absolute and there is no time limit.

4.49 Whether the club owns its premises on a freehold basis or holds then under a lease, it will need to have trustees. These persons will hold the freehold or the leasehold on behalf of the members of the club. The reason for this has already been explained: see paras. 1.51 and 3.5, above.

4.50 A tenancy is usually created by a formal document (a "lease"). The lease not only gives the Club a right to the land; it also creates contractual obligations which bind both the landlord and the tenant. These are called "covenants". It is important that the club's trustees and committee are aware of their obligations under the lease, since a breach of a covenant may cause the club's lease to be subject to forfeiture by the landlord. This means that the lease is terminated.

4.51 This section will concentrate on covenants and the consequences of a breach of covenant. In other words, it will look at the obligations owed by the club as a lessee of land to its landlord. It will not look at other matters, such as the consequences of granting leases of parts of the club's premises.

Covenants

4.52 The lease of premises granted to the club will contain express covenants. Put simply, a covenant is a promise to do something; the lease will contain separate covenants binding both the landlord and the tenant. If the lease does not expressly deal with a specific matter, then there will be a question whether a covenant may be implied into the lease. The covenants most likely to be found in a lease are:

- a covenant to pay rent;
- a covenant to pay taxes such as council tax; and
- a covenant to maintain the premises in appropriate repair.

Covenants commonly found in leases relate to matters such as:
- assignment of the lease by the tenant;
- carrying on of trades and activities; and
- carrying out repairs.

The term "assignment of the lease" means transferring the tenancy to a new tenant. In that case, the rights and obligations are transferred from the old tenant to the new.

4.53 In the event of a covenant being broken, the landlord has the right of forfeiture. This means that the landlord has the right to terminate the tenancy. As this remedy is a powerful weapon, the landlord's right to forfeit the lease is qualified by a number of restrictions. These include procedural requirements which the landlord needs to follow. In addition, the tenant has extensive rights to apply to the court for relief against forfeiture.

4.54 Bearing in mind the complexity of this area of the law, a club which finds itself in dispute with its landlord should go to its lawyers for advice.

Other non-criminal liability

4.55 The other areas of law likely to affect a club are:

- employment rights; and
- unlawful discrimination

4.56 The club as an employer may incur liability under employment law in relation to its employees. Employees are employed under a contract of employment and so have rights under their contract. More important, they have a large number of statutory rights. These arise both during their employment and upon termination of their employment. They are set out at paras. 4.58 to 4.76 below.

4.57 So far as possible liability for unlawful discriminations is concerned, the club may incur liability in relation to three groups:

- its members;
- its employees; and
- guests to its premises

This area of possible liability is looked at in paras. 4.77 to 4.92.

Employment rights

4.58 Employees have an extensive array of basic statutory rights. Many of them arise during their employment. But they also have rights in relation to dismissal, particularly the statutory right not to be unfairly dismissed. These rights arise under the Employment Rights Act 1996. The Act has been subject to substantial amendment over the years since its enactment and will be further amended by legislation currently before Parliament – the Employment Rights Bill. The Bill is expected to be enacted in July and to come into effect in the autumn. Clubs with employees will be affected by its provisions and should take steps to ensure they are alerted to its implementation date.

4.59 At the outset, it should be made clear that the most significant statutory rights are given to employees. Some rights are given to a group called "workers". If a person is neither an employee nor a worker, then they will not have any of the statutory rights and will probably be self-employed. But – confusingly – some self-employed persons may be workers. The law relating to defining these groups is complex.

4.60 It is likely that a club will use the services of a number of different groups of staff:

- employees
- "consultants"
- agency workers

Most of the staff to be found in a club are probably employees and, in relation to them, the club will need to ensure that those running it are aware of their employees' statutory rights. A large club will probably employ a Secretary or Chief Executive who may be expected to be aware of the club's statutory obligations. They club may also employ a Human Resources Manager.

Consultants

4.61 The club may also use the services of "consultants" to carry out certain jobs on the premises but in circumstances where it is not necessary to have them there on a full-time basis. For example, they may called upon to sort out problems with the club's IT system as and when they arise. The term "consultant" denotes someone who is self-employed and provides their services on that basis. They may also, though, be workers. If they are classified as such, the club may also have some statutory obligations to them.

Distinction between employees and consultants

4.62 The distinction between employees and consultants (i.e. self-employed/workers) has been litigated regularly in the employment tribunals and courts over the years. Even before the introduction of statutory rights, the distinction was important. For example, an employer owes a duty of care to its employees but not to self-employed people working on its premises. At that time, disputes arose where a person suffered an accident or industrial injury. If the victim was an employee, the employer would be liable to pay compensation; if not, the "employer" would not be liable. The 1960s saw the enactment of the first statutory rights and, in the years since then, they have increased in volume.

4.63 A question arises as to whether someone is an employee or not, the starting-point for the discussion is the question posed by the court in *Ready Mixed Concrete (South East) v Minister of Pensions and Social Security* (1968): "Is the worker in business on his own account?" To answer that question all the relevant factors need to be considered.

Distinction between employees and workers

4.64 All employees are workers and so they have all the statutory rights given to employees, as well as the statutory rights given to workers. An example of such rights is the right to holidays and holiday pay. Those who have successfully claimed to be workers have been self-employed taxi drivers working for Uber and delivery drivers for courier companies.

Agency workers

4.65 The other group of staff likely to be used by a club are agency workers. These will probably be used when the club has a function for which it needs extra staff. Agency workers are provided by an agency and it is the agency with whom the worker has a contract. There is no contract of any sort between the club and the agency worker.

Rights during employment

4.66 The most significant rights given to an employee are:

- rights in relation to "whistleblowing"

- the right to time off work for various purposes
- the right to parental and adoption leave
- the right to flexible working

These rights are extensive and are likely to be added to by the legislation currently before Parliament. An employee who claims a breach of one or more of the rights has the right to take a case to an employment tribunal.

Rights in relation to dismissal

4.67 An employee who is dismissed is likely to have the following rights:

- the right to claim breach of contract
- the statutory right to claim unfair dismissal
- the statutory right to a redundancy payment

Breach of contract

4.68 A breach of contract claim is likely to be available to an employee who was dismissed without notice or with less notice than they were entitled to under their contract. A claim for breach of contract is also known as a *wrongful dismissal* claim. In reality, the employee(s) most likely to claim wrongful dismissal will be those on the club's staff who are either highly paid and/or have a long period of notice. In other words, they will be people such as the secretary and other senior staff, such as an Accounts Manager or Human Resources Manager. Other staff will be most likely to claim unfair dismissal in the employment tribunal. Breach of contract claims are decided by the County Court or High Court (depending on the amount of compensation claimed).

Unfair dismissal

4.69 The statutory right not to be unfairly dismissed arises under the Employment Rights Act 1996. Claims are made in the employment tribunal, as previously mentioned. The focus of an unfair dismissal claim is likely to be on the reason for the dismissal and the way the dismissal was handled. The Act sets out five reasons which an employer may rely on in relation to the dismissal:

1. Capability
2. Conduct
3. Redundancy
4. Contravention of an enactment
5. "Some other substantial reason of a kind such as to justify the dismissal of an employee holding the position which the employee held".

See section 98(1).

4.70 The usual reasons for a dismissal are the first two. In relation to the third – redundancy – the point to note here is that, even if the employer has to deal with a redundancy situation, it is still obliged to go about the necessary dismissals reasonably. An example of the fourth reason is the situation where a delivery driver is banned from driving and thus cannot drive without committing a crime under the Road Traffic legislation.

4.71 Once the employer has established the reason for the dismissal, it needs to ensure that it goes through a fair procedure before dismissing the employee. This is because of section 98(4) of the Act, which states:

"Where the employer has fulfilled the requirements of subsection (1), the determination of the question whether the dismissal is fair or unfair (having regard to the reason shown by the employer)—

(a) depends on whether in the circumstances (including the size and administrative resources of the employer's undertaking) the employer acted reasonably or unreasonably in treating it as a sufficient reason for dismissing the employee, and

(b) shall be determined in accordance with equity and the substantial merits of the case."

4.72 The following points should be noted from section 98(4) above:

- The employer needs to establish a reason for the dismissal
- That reason must be 'sufficient'
- Whether the dismissal was fair or not depends on a number of factors:

      o   the circumstances surrounding the dismissal

      o   the 'size and administrative resources' of the undertaking

- In deciding whether the employer's decision to dismiss was reasonable, the employment tribunal will decide the claim 'in accordance with equity and the substantial merits of the case'.

4.73 The factors set out in the preceding paragraph give the employment tribunal flexibility in dealing with claims. A larger club may be expected to have larger resources than a smaller club. So, in dealing with a dismissal issue it will be expected to have a more elaborate apparatus for dealing with the matter, including an internal appeal mechanism which the employee can use. But what needs to be emphasised is that, however good a reason the employer thinks it has for dismissing the employee, there will be few cases when it will be able to justify an instant dismissal without going through some sort of internal process. Even if it suspects the employee to be guilty of a crime, it is better that it should go through a procedure before dismissing the employee.

4.74 In the case of redundancy, it is not enough for the employer to proceed to dismissal of staff without going through an appropriate process. Whilst redundancy may be a perfectly good reason for dismissing some of the employees, it does not absolve the employer from handling the process fairly.

4.75 A factor of particular relevance in the context of an unfair dismissal claim against a club by a member of its staff is the treatment of the staff by members of the club. The club members are not the employers of the staff. Liability for their dismissal will lie with the committee, who are treated as the employer. This is because the club has no legal personality and, therefore, cannot be treated in law as the employer. Nevertheless, if in the context of an unfair dismissal claim, it emerges that the employee was subjected to abusive or unpleasant treatment by one or more of the members, that treatment will be one of the 'circumstances' (as set out in s.98(4)) which the tribunal will take into account. For that reason, it is advisable – as mentioned in para. 2.99 - that the club should have a procedure for dealing with complaints relating to members' behaviour.

Right to a redundancy payment

4.76 A claim for a redundancy payment is a separate claim from the claim for unfair dismissal. In practice, though, an employee dismissed for redundancy – whether or not he/she has received a redundancy payment – is likely to claim unfair dismissal. The basis of the claim would be that, although the employer's reason for the dismissal was redundancy – and thus one of the reasons set out in s.98 – the way the employer went about dismissing the employee in that redundancy situation was unreasonable and thus was in breach of section 98(4).

Unlawful discrimination

4.77 Unlawful discrimination was discussed in Chapter 2, in relation to applicants for membership of the club and members: see paras. 2.20 (and following paragraphs, in relation to applicants) and 2.43 (and following paragraphs, in relation to members). Cases of unlawful discrimination pose particular problems for an organisation and clubs need to take care in this respect. Litigation involving claims of unlawful discrimination can be lengthy and time-consuming and the publicity generated uncomfortable. In addition, compensation for unlawful discrimination has no financial limit set upon it. So the club is exposed to potentially high awards of compensation, although, in reality, high awards of compensation in successful discrimination claims are fairly rare, despite the newspaper headlines they generate. By contrast, in most cases of unfair dismissal there is a limit to the amount of compensation that a tribunal may award against an employer.

4.78 It is important to note that a club may also be a *service provider* in addition to being an "association" within the meaning of the Equality Act. This would happen, for example, if a golf club opened its golf course, café and shop to members of the public on certain days of the week. Another example is a club which makes its facilities available for weddings. In respect of *these* activities, the club is a service provider. That means that any liability which arises in relation to the provision of such services falls within different parts of the Act *in relation to the provision of those services.* Someone who uses the club's services and claims to have suffered unlawful discrimination will make a claim under other provisions of the Act. The provisions being considered here are those relating to "associations", that is clubs.

4.79 In this chapter, the club's liability for unlawful discrimination is discussed in relation to the following groups:

- the club's members;
- the club's staff; and
- visitors to the club and guests/prospective guests to the club

4.80 The main provisions of the Equality Act 2010 were discussed in Chapter 2: see para. 2.23 to 2.31. In brief, a person claiming unlawful discrimination needs to establish two things:

- that he/she has a "protected characteristic"; and
- that he/she was discriminated against because of that characteristic.

There are four categories of discrimination:

1. direct discrimination;
2. indirect discrimination;
3. victimisation; and
4. harassment.

Club members

4.81 As we saw in Chapter 2, the club may incur liability in the following ways:

- In relation to candidates for membership of the club: see para. 2.20
- In relation to the treatment of members: see para. 2.43

The second category includes taking away membership, varying the terms of membership and subjecting the member to "any other detriment": see section 101(2). Since discrimination in relation to club members was discussed fully in Chapter 2, it is only included here for the sake of completeness. Note that a complaint of discrimination in relation to membership of a club must be brought in the county court.

Club staff

4.82 A discrimination claim is likely to arise in three possible situations:

1. recruitment of staff
2. treatment of staff
3. dismissal of staff

Recruitment

4.83 The Equality Act makes it unlawful to discriminate against applicants in three ways:

- in the recruitment arrangements;
- in the terms offered to the successful candidate; and
- by not offering the job to a candidate.

See section 39(1). In all three cases a candidate could make a claim if the reason for the discrimination was that he/she had a protected characteristic.

Treatment of staff

4.84 Section 39(2) of the Act makes it unlawful to discriminate against an existing member of staff (B) in the following ways:

- in relation to terms of employment;
- in the way the employer gives B access to opportunities:
  - ○ for promotion, transfer or training; or
  - ○ for receiving any other benefit, facility or service;
- by not giving B access to such opportunities;
- by dismissing B; and
- by subjecting B to any other detriment.

Examples of this last type of unlawful discrimination are:

- unwanted conduct (for example, harassment) by a club member or club officer; or
- ostracisation from a group or activity by supervising club staff and/or fellow club employees.

Victimisation

4.85 The provisions of the Act relating to victimisation – section 39(3) and (4) – are in similar terms to those relating to recruitment and treatment of staff.

4.86 As with unfair dismissal claims – see para. 4.69 above – claims relating to discrimination in employment are heard in the employment tribunal.

Club visitors and guests/prospective guests

4.87 The Act also embraces other people, particularly those who use the club but who are not full members of it. The two categories of such people are:

1.   temporary or associate members; and
2.   guests or prospective guests.

Those in *both* categories are third parties in relation to whom the club may incur liability. An associate or guest who wishes to complain of unlawful discrimination must bring their claim in the county court.

4.88 Those in the first category above are called by the Act "associates". It defines an associate as:

(a) a person who is not a member of the club; but
(b) who has some or all of the rights as a member because of their membership of another club.

See section 107(6). This definition includes visitors from other clubs with which the club has reciprocal arrangements.

4.89 Those in the second category (above) may be either:

- guests of a full member of the club;
- guests of temporary or associate members; or
- prospective guests.

Associates

4.90 The provisions of the Act apply to associates in the same way as they apply to members of the club. So, it is unlawful to discriminate against an associate in the following ways:

- in the way he or she is given access, or denied access, to a benefit, facility or service;
- by varying the terms of the associate's membership; or
- by subjecting them to any other detriment.

See section 101(3). Associates are also protected against harassment and victimisation: see s. 101(4) and (7).

Guests

4.91 Guests are treated in a similar way: see section 102. The harassment provisions only apply to the protected characteristics of age, disability, gender reassignment, race and sex: see s. 103(2). The Government Guidance gives examples of the operation of these provisions. Two of them are worth noting here. The first relates to a member of a university alumni association who invites a transsexual guest to its annual dinner. During the course of his speech the president makes remarks about transsexual people which upset the guest. This is unlawful harassment of the guest related to gender reassignment. The second example relates to a guest who is refused service in the club because she is a Muslim. She brings a successful claim against the club for discrimination on the grounds of religion or belief. On her next visit to the club as a guest she is denied access because she brought a claim against the club. This is an example of unlawful victimisation.

Prospective guests

4.92 A prospective guest is someone who would be a guest but for the fact that they are prevented from being a guest by the club's rules because of a protected characteristic. For example, a club is holding its annual dinner. The spouses/partners of members are also invited to the dinner as guests of the club. The partner of one member is black and is not invited because the organisers believe that other members and their guests will object. This is direct associative discrimination on racial grounds against the member because of his association with his partner. It would also be direct discrimination against a prospective guest, since the partner is not invited because of the organisers' belief in relation to the other members and their guests. Consequently, the partner will also have a claim under the Act. (This example is taken from the Equality and Human Rights Commission's Guidance. See https://www.equalityhumanrights.com/equality/equality-act-2010/equality-act-2010-guiding-principles-associations.)

Health and safety

4.93 The Health and Safety at Work Act 1974 (HSAWA), as amended by later legislation – together with the numerous Regulations published in connection with it – generally imposes *criminal liability* on employers who fall foul of its provisions. Broadly speaking the duties imposed by the Act are similar to the employer's obligations in relation to negligence and occupier's liability: see paras. 4.35 and 4.41 above.

Duties

4.94 In general terms, all employers have a duty of care under HASAWA. All employers, whatever the size of the business, must:

- make the workplace safe and prevent risks to health; and
- make sure that plant and machinery is safe to use.

Accordingly, a club, as an employer, should:

- prepare a health and safety policy;
- manage risks and risk assessment at work;
- report any accidents and illness;
- provide information and training;
- consult with its employees/workers on safety issues;
- ensure it has First Aid in work; and
- display health and safety information on its premises.

See: www.hse.gov.uk/simple-health-safety.

Liabilities

4.95 The Act and the numerous regulations implemented under it do not give rise to civil liability. In other words breaches of the legislation are dealt with in the criminal courts, not the civil courts. But they are relevant in relation to determining the standard of care required of an employer. In summary, the duties of an employer – both under the ordinary law and the Act and Regulations – are to provide:

- a safe place of work
- a safe system of work
- safe equipment and materials
- competent fellow-employees.

4.96 The club should maintain insurance against liability for bodily injury or diseases sustained by employees arising out of and in the course of their employment. The sum insured must not be less than £5 million in respect of any one occurrence. The insurer's annual certificate must be displayed in the clubhouse and be easily seen and read by every person employed there. These obligations are imposed by the Employers' Liability (Compulsory Insurance) Act 1969 and the Employers' Liability (Compulsory Insurance) Regulations 1998.

Remedies

4.97 The Health and Safety Executive (HSE) is the UK's statutory enforcement body for ensuring prevention of accidents and for maintaining good standards in health and safety. However, it will, where appropriate, enforce the law where it finds that safety laws are being deliberately flouted and will take enforcement action to ensure that duty holders:

- deal immediately with serious risks (so they prevent harm);
- comply with the law; and/or
- are held to account if they fail in their responsibilities.

Individuals may bring claims before the courts for personal injury.

Criminal liability

Introduction

4.98 It is not possible to go into all the possible situations which may give rise to criminal liability. Only those most likely to affect a club are looked at here. They are liability under:

- the Licensing Act 2003;
- the Food Safety Act 1990 and the Food Safety and Hygiene (England) Regulations 2013; and
- the Health Act 2006 in relation to smoking on the club's premises.

There are numerous other pieces of legislation which may affect a club. The question in all cases where there is alleged criminal liability is: *who* should be prosecuted?

4.99 It is clear that a club is capable of being prosecuted. What is less clear is *who* should be prosecuted. There are three groups to be considered for prosecution in a case where a crime is alleged to have been committed. The prosecutor may bring a prosecution against:

1. the club;
2. the officers of the club; or
3. the members of the club.

The two main cases to have considered this question are *R v RL and JF* (2008) (the *RL case*) and *R v Lear and Lear* (2018) (the *Lear case*). The first arose under the Water Resources Act 1991 and involved a leakage oil from a golf club's storage tank which polluted a nearby watercourse. The second arose under the Health and Safety at Work Act 1974 and involved the death of a hotel guest who fell out a sash window because of a lack of maintenance of the window. Unfortunately, these cases do not establish any clear rule about who should be prosecuted. This is because, as the Court of Appeal said in the *RL case*, there is no general rule as to who should be prosecuted. So, the Act of Parliament under which a prosecution is brought has to be looked at to see who may be prosecuted.

4.100 Some Acts relating to the criminal liability of unincorporated bodies such as clubs contain an "officers' liability clause". This is a provision which extends liability to individual officers in certain cases. If the Act contains such a clause then it will be clear that in specified cases the officers or members of the governing body of the club may be prosecuted in respect of the aiding and abetting, or the conniving, of an offence or because of some neglect on their part.

4.101 Although there are suggestions in the *RL case* that it is appropriate to prosecute all the members of the club, it is more likely that in most cases the officers of the club would be prosecuted rather than all the members.

Vicarious liability

4.102 As we saw in relation to civil liability, vicarious liability may arise in relation to the activities of the club's staff. Clearly, there will be no vicarious liability for a member of the staff who commits a crime which has nothing to do with the club – for example, an act of theft. On the other hand, the club will be vicariously liable for a member of staff who commits a criminal act in the course of his or her employment.

4.103 Many of the cases which have dealt with this issue have arisen in the context of licensing and have considered whether a licensee of premises is liable for breach of the Licensing legislation. What usually happens is that the licensee delegates the running of the premises to an employee and the employee commits the crime which gives rise to the prosecution. In relation to the vicarious liability of the licensee, the question is whether he/she *knew* that the crime was being committed. It is clear that the core question the courts will ask is not whether the licensee *actually* knew but whether he/she may be taken to have known. The case of *Linnett v Metropolitan Police Commissioner* (1946) involved an absentee licensee of a pub who was convicted of "knowingly permitting disorderly conduct" where he had left control of the premises to someone else, who had in fact knowingly permitted the conduct complained of. The Lord Chief Justice, Lord Goddard CJ, said:

> "If the manager chooses to delegate the carrying on of the business to another, whether or not that other is his [employee], then what that other does or what he knows must be imputed to the person who put the other into that position."

4.104 The upshot of these cases is that the club's committee needs to put in place procedures for making sure that the activities being carried on at the club are properly managed and supervised. If they do so, they will be able to defend themselves against an argument that they are vicariously liable.

Sale of alcohol

4.105 The Licensing Act 2003 governs this area of the club's activities. Under the Act, the offences which may be committed are called "unauthorised licensable activities" and are to be found in Part 7 of the Act. Section 139 provides a defence of "due diligence".

Food safety law

4.106 The Food Safety Act and the Food Safety and Hygiene (England) Regulations 2013 establish various offences relating to the sale and supply of food. As with the Licensing Act, a defence of due diligence is available.

Smoking

4.107 The Health Act 2006 bans smoking in public places and workplaces. It is clear that its provisions affect clubs. The provisions of the Act are fleshed out in the Smoke-free (Premises and Enforcement) Regulations 2006.

Other criminal liability

4.108 As can be seen from discussion at the beginning of this section, there are numerous Acts and Regulations which may affect a club and of which it may unwittingly fall foul. It is impossible to list them all.

A GUIDE TO CLUB LAW AND PRACTICE

Appendix

Club Rules

The Table below sets out the sorts of Rules which a club may have. Bearing in mind that one size does not fit all, and that a large club will need a more elaborate set of rules than a small club, it would not be appropriate to set out model rules. The rules below offer suggestions as to what sorts of rules may be included and how they might be drafted. The relevant paragraphs of the book are **cross-referenced.**

Rule		Matters to be considered	Comments	Paragraph no.
Name of Club/Association				
Objects and purposes		Identify main and subsidiary objects of the club	1. The objects should be drafted sufficiently widely so as to allow for future developments or changes. 2. If the club is a sports club the sports should be defined and there should be a reference to the rules of the governing body of the sport(s) in question.	1.18 - 1.24
Categories of members	General	Consider the following matters: • Limits on numbers in each category • Qualifications for each category • Definitions, e.g. "overseas" • Different voting rights for each category • Restrictions on club usage, e.g. for overseas members	1. The club does not need to use all the categories of membership listed here. 2. For each category appropriate criteria for election to the category should be set out. 3. If appropriate the class should be	2.6 – 2.19

Rule			Matters to be considered	Comments	Paragraph no.
		•	Eligibility for election as Committee member or office	defined, e.g. "overseas".	
	Full/Ordinary Social Overseas Temporary Associate Junior Honorary Life		See above remarks.		2.11 2.12 2.13 2.14 2.15 2.16 2.18 2.19
Election/Admission of members		• • - - - - - •	Procedure for admission or election delegated to Committee Procedure should set out, e.g. Proposer/seconder Standing of proposer and seconder, e.g. minimum length of membership Interview by committee member(s) Requirement to show ability to play sport (if applicable) Number of adverse votes in committee to defeat election On election, member to be subject to Rules	1. Rules should cater for method of election to each category of member. 2. Express rule stating that members are subject to the Rules is useful. 3. Admission procedure should comply with Equality Act 2010	2.8 1.45 – 1.46 2.20 – 2.42
Members' dues	Entrance fee Annual subscription	• • • •	Newly elected members not entitled to rights etc of membership until entrance fee paid Non-payment of entrance fee may lead to suspension or termination of membership Method of payment of annual subscription, e.g. in instalments Rules should set out a procedure for dealing with non-payment of annual subscription	1. An entrance fee is not essential but, if there is one, the rules should set out the consequences of non-payment by new member. 2. The Rules should deal with consequences of non-payment of dues by all members. 3. The procedure for dealing with non-	2.85 – 2.89 2.85 – 2.89 2.80

Rule		Matters to be considered	Comments	Paragraph no.
			payment of dues should be separate from the disciplinary procedure.	
Officers	General	For all officers, rules should deal with the following: • Method of selection • Duration of tenure • Role – if any – in the management of the club	The question of the role in the management of the club arises mainly in relation to the offices of President and Vice-President.	3.10 – 3.16
	President Vice-President(s) (if any)			3.10 – 3.13
	Chairman	• Method of election • Duration of office • Powers to act on behalf of Committee	1. The Chairman may be elected: • By the members at the AGM • By the Committee 2. Consider what express powers the Chairman should be given, e.g. the power to enter into contracts with third parties.	3.17 – 3.20 3.61 3.49, 3.78, 3.81
	Secretary	• Whether a paid secretary is necessary • Consider what express powers (if any) to give him/her, e.g. power to enter into contracts with third parties.	1. A larger club – particularly one with premises – should appoint a paid Secretary. 2. He/she will be an employee and should not be a member of the club. 3. He/she should have a contract of employment. 4. In relation to express powers, the issue is the same as with the	3.21 – 3.23 3.21 3.21 3.23, 3.49, 3.78, 3.81

Rule			Matters to be considered	Comments	Paragraph no.
				powers (if any) given to the Chairman	
				5. In a small club he/she will be honorary (i.e. unpaid)	
	Treasurer	•	Whether the treasurer should be an employee or unpaid (honorary)	1. This depends on the size of the club. A large club may need a paid accountant or an accounts department. 2. If the post of Treasurer is honorary, there should be a rule requiring him/her to be a member of the Club.	3.24 – 3.26
Trustees		• • •	Method of election Duration of office Role in management of club, e.g. - attendance at Committee meetings - power to vote at such meetings	1. This group is separate from the officers. 2. They are not usually involved in the running of the club. 3. The club's property is put into their name.	3.5 – 3.9 1.53, 3.9 1.51 – 1.53
Management and Running of the Club	Committee	• • •	The Rules should deal with the method of selection of the Committee Rules should set out how the Committee is to operate. They should deal with the following: - Composition - Operation - Method of selection - Meetings of the Committee - Attendance at meetings - Minutes of meetings	1. There should be *express* rules dealing with the method of selection and the operation of the Committee. 2. Two groups of powers need to be set out: - Powers relating to the operation of the club - Powers relating to dealings with third parties.	3.37 and 3.27 3.59 – 3.72 and 3.73 – 94

Rule		Matters to be considered	Comments	Paragraph no.
		- Duties - Powers	3. Consider whether the business of the Committee may be conducted *electronically*, particularly - Whether the *meetings* may be conducted using electronic means, e.g. Zoom etc; - Whether the *business of the committee* may be conducted using electronic means, e.g. email. 4. Consider whether the minutes of Committee meetings should be available to members. 5. There should be a rule indemnifying members of the Committee in the event of liability: see below.	3.47 – 3.48 See also 3.119 which has a model rule for dealing with club meetings. 2.60 3.99
	Sub-Committees	• The rules should set out the Committee's powers in relation to sub-committees. • The rules should deal with the operation of sub-committees, e.g. requirement to report to Committee.		3.35, 3.50, 3.63 – 3.65
	Co-option to committee and sub-committees	• The rules should give the Committee a power of co-option.		3.34, 3.62 – 3.63
	Power to make byelaws/regulations	• There should be a power to make byelaws or regulations to deal with the day-to-day running of the Club.	1. The power to make byelaws/regulations gives flexibility to the Committee	3.66 – 3.71

Rule		Matters to be considered	Comments	Paragraph no.
			in the day to-day running of the Club and avoids the necessity for calling a General Meeting. 2. The regulations may cover matters such as - Power to raise subscriptions - Opening hours of bar and restaurant (if any) - Dress codes - Treatment of staff by members - Associate members and guests.	
	Power to fill casual vacancies		This is a useful power.	3.72
Declarations of Interest			It is important for a committee member to make a declaration of interest in case a conflict arises between his/her personal interest and the club's interest. This is important in relation to the Club's dealings with third parties, e.g. contractors.	3.77
Indemnity			Such a rule indemnifies Committee members against claims made against them in connection with the proper discharge of their duties. See above.	3.99 - 3.100

Rule		Matters to be considered	Comments	Paragraph no.
Additional Financial Powers		Consider whether the Committee should have the following powers: • To impose a levy on members to defray an item of expenditure • To set up and maintain a sinking or reserve fund • Powers of investment • Power to reimburse expenditure incurred by committee members	Such a rule is linked with the Indemnity rule, above.	
Communications		• Rule to require members to keep club up-to-date with personal details • Communications by club with membership: - Method of communication to members - Communication of notices to members - Consequences of non-arrival or late arrival of notices - Electronic communications	1. Need for awareness of the requirements of the Data Protection legislation. 2. Rules need to deal with method of communication to members, e.g. electronic communications 3. It is important for the Rules to deal with problems with communication of notices to members to avoid arguments about the validity of a General Meeting.	2.47 – 2.64 2.44 – 2.46 2.46
Membership List		• Rules should make clear Club's right to hold personal details • Rules should deal with accessibility of personal details to other members	Rules need to address issues of members' access to data and the club's membership lists.	2.56 – 2.64
Resignation of members		• Rule should state whether writing required and when resignation should be submitted to be valid	Important to have a rule dealing with members' resignations for the sake of clarity.	2.120 – 2.124

APPENDIX

Rule		Matters to be considered	Comments	Paragraph no.
		• No particular form of words required.		
Breaches of the Rules		• There should be a rule stating what amounts to a breach of the Rules.	1. This sort of rule should be linked with the Club's Disciplinary Procedure. 2. In the absence of such a rule, there would be a risk of the procedure being invalid.	2.79, 2.90 – 2.92
Disciplinary procedure	General matters	The following matters should be included: • What events may trigger the procedure • Who may initiate the procedure • The form of the procedure • Sanctions which may be applied • Appeals	1. The procedure should be flexible and should cater for both minor and major breaches and single and multiple breaches by a member. 2. A large club will need a more elaborate procedure than a small one.	2.79 – 2.84 2.93 – 2.119
	Breaches of the rules		Breaches may be minor or serious and may occur once or regularly.	2.90 – 2.92
	Initiation of the procedure	• Consider who may initiate - The committee? - A group of members?		2.97 – 2.100
	Form of the procedure	The following should be dealt with: • Notice to member of charges and opportunity to respond • Constitution of group to deal with matter • Nature of hearing – confined to writing? • Legal representation?	1. The matters mentioned here should be dealt with in the rules. 2. Time limits should be set for each stage of the procedure.	2.101 – 2.108
	Sanction	Consider the following: • Fine • Reprimand/warning/censure	1. Flexibility is needed to cater for different types of breach.	2.109 – 2.115

Rule		Matters to be considered	Comments	Paragraph no.
		• Suspension, including - Length - Nature of member's rights during suspension • Expulsion - Requirements for a valid decision to expel	2. In the case of a decision to expel a member, the rules should set out how the decision to expel should be arrived at, e.g. by a bare majority of the Committee or a two thirds majority.	
	Appeals	• Nature of appeal – review or re-hearing? • Constitution of appeal panel • Powers of appeal panel	1. The role of an appeal panel is usually to review the integrity of the original hearing. 2. In a larger club – particularly one with a disciplinary function – a more elaborate appeal process may be needed.	2.116 – 2.119
Meetings	Generally	• Business to be conducted • Notice requirements • Agenda • Attendance and quorum • Motions • Conduct of the meeting • Voting • Minutes • Electronic meetings	It is important for the Rules to cater for meetings to be conducted electronically.	3.102 – 3.104, 3.105 – 3.139
	Annual General Meetings (AGMs)			3.105 – 3.139
	Special Meetings (EGMs)	• The Rules should specify: - Minimum number of signatures for a requisition - Amount of notice of meeting - Number of members required to be present		3.140 – 3.145

Rule		Matters to be considered	Comments	Paragraph no.
		- Motion to be debated at meeting - Voting requirements in relation to motion		
	Procedure at meetings		The role of the Chairman is important.	3.120 – 3.136
Guests and Visitors		• Rule for introduction of guests and visitors to the Club, e.g. - Member to be responsible for behaviour of guests - Power to Committee to exclude		
Interpretation of the Rules				1.42 – 1.44
Amendment of the Rules		• The procedure for changing the rules should be set out, e.g. - notice requirements - size of majority required	1. There should be a rule allowing the rules to be changed 2. The rules should contain a procedure for dealing with rule changes 3. An EGM is usually used for such a purpose	1.34 – 1.41
Dispute Resolution			The purpose of such a rule is to enable disputes to be resolved without recourse to litigation and the inevitable unwelcome publicity.	2.125 – 2.129
Dissolution of the Club		• There should be a procedure for dissolving the club.	1. The procedure should involve an EGM with appropriate notice requirements. 2. The procedure should include a method of dealing with surplus assets on dissolution.	1.155 – 1.161

Rule		Matters to be considered	Comments	Paragraph no.
			3. The distribution of the assets need not be to surviving members but may be to other organisation.	

Index

www.ingramcontent.com/pod-product-compliance
Lightning Source LLC
Chambersburg PA
CBHW071643210326
41597CB00017B/2093